for Retirement

SET YOUR DESTINATION
& ENJOY THE JOURNEY

MARK FRIED

Advantage®

Published by Advantage, Charleston, South Carolina.
Member of Advantage Media Group.

ADVANTAGE is a registered trademark, and the Advantage colophon is a trademark of Advantage Media Group, Inc.

Printed in the United States of America.

10 9 8 7 6 5 4 3 2 1

ISBN: 978-1-59932-797-6
LCCN: 2017939678

Cover design by George Stevens.
Layout design by Katie Biondo.

This publication is designed to provide accurate and authoritative information in regard to the subject matter covered. It is sold with the understanding that the publisher is not engaged in rendering legal, accounting, or other professional services. If legal advice or other expert assistance is required, the services of a competent professional person should be sought.

Advantage Media Group is proud to be a part of the Tree Neutral® program. Tree Neutral offsets the number of trees consumed in the production and printing of this book by taking proactive steps such as planting trees in direct proportion to the number of trees used to print books. To learn more about Tree Neutral, please visit **www.treeneutral.com**.

Advantage Media Group is a publisher of business, self-improvement, and professional development books. We help entrepreneurs, business leaders, and professionals share their Stories, Passion, and Knowledge to help others Learn & Grow. Do you have a manuscript or book idea that you would like us to consider for publishing? Please visit **advantagefamily.com** or call **1.866.775.1696**.

Table of Contents

Acknowledgments

First and most importantly, to my wife, Alexis. As we reach our twenty-fourth year of marriage, I think back to the end of our first year of marriage, when my mother asked Alexis how it felt to be married a whole year. Alexis replied that it felt like five years. There are many ups and downs that we all face in life. I couldn't ask for a better wife, partner, and friend to stand by my side.

To my children, Steven and Carly, now almost all grown up. Thanks for understanding that sometimes, I had to go into the office or visit a client or call on a prospect even though I would have much rather been spending more time with you.

To my parents, who shared so many lessons with me about life. Sometimes it takes a decade or two to have that "aha!" moment when it all comes together.

To Lisa and my team at TFG Wealth Management, who help make all that magic happen every day and who understand that we are on a mission to help people and make lives better.

To all the mentors and friends throughout the years who have shared their insights into the world of finance and the world in general. To my clients, whom I consider family, for helping me enrich my life by giving me the privilege of helping them.

I also want to thank my editor Bob Sheasley and all the folks at Advantage Media Group who helped get me over the finish line.

Preface

I n my workshops and in this book, I'm not selling or recommending any type of investment. You will not be reading about some next, best investment idea. Instead, I will be telling you about concepts that are crucial to understand when making the big decisions about your financial future. Comprehensive financial planning involves a variety of elements, and by the end of this book, you will have a strong grasp of what you need to know as you prepare for a prosperous retirement.

This book was created to be read from beginning to end. Concepts discussed in each chapter will be built upon as you move through this book.

Each chapter starts out with a brief overview of what will be discussed and ends with a series of questions for your consideration. The purpose of these questions is to get you thinking about the issues and risks you will face in the future. If you are serious about preparing for retirement, you will make every effort to answer these questions.

I also strongly suggest you read this book with a highlighter in hand. I have packed each chapter with a lot of ideas and concepts;

however, they won't all apply to you. You can use the highlighter to mark issues or concepts that you feel are important to look at, given your personal situation.

Disclaimer: The author and publisher have used their best efforts in preparing this book. It is not intended to offer specific financial, legal, or tax advice. Your financial goals and circumstances are unique. You should consult with a financial professional, tax professional, and legal professional before implementing any of the concepts discussed in this book.

Introduction

LESSONS TO SHARE

Alone in the house where I grew up in Margate, New Jersey, I finally had time to reflect. I'd gone back to put my mother's affairs in order after her passing, and I couldn't stop thinking about something she told me after doctors discovered the cancer that soon would take her life.

Hedva Fried was a first-grade teacher for thirty-seven years—long enough to see some of her earliest pupils become grandparents. It seemed she knew everybody. After she retired, and a few years after my father, Harris, died, she decided to take her dream trip to China. She had long wanted to see the Terracotta Army of antiquity.

She and my father hadn't been able to travel after he had a heart attack and stroke at age sixty. He lived for a decade after that, but they hadn't ventured far from home. My mother devoted herself to helping take care of him until his death in July of 2001.

At seventy-two, my mother looked forward to the day in October when she would begin her journey. She felt fit and in good shape—an avid tennis player who often rode her bike around town. In August, however, she started to feel a worsening pain in her hip. She went to her doctor, and then to specialists, who discovered her cancer. It was Stage IV. It had metastasized.

The doctors at Fox Chase Cancer Center in Philadelphia were uncertain of the exact nature of the cancer, but they did advise us that it had spread and that her situation was grim. The treatment, they said, would depend upon the results of a PET scan, although they doubted any treatment could help her.

When facing the loss of a loved one, even the slightest chance seems worth pursuing. My mother's health insurance would not pay for the scan, because the cancer was so advanced and because the doctors agreed that no treatment would save her life. This was an expensive test.

After the doctors left the room, my mother called me to her side and said, "I don't know if I can afford it, Mark."

A few months later, in my grief, those were the words that kept coming back to me as I sat there at the dining room table in Margate. I had made sure she got that test, despite the cost, but the doctors had been correct. She had died within a few months, in January of 2004.

As I pondered the situation, I wondered why she had even questioned whether she should get the test. Why was she so worried about money? What made her think she needed to scrimp on a matter of life and death?

While organizing her papers, I started looking at her assets and investments. My mother had been working with a stockbroker at a large brokerage firm, and I concluded that he had given her horrible advice. The investments had poor returns and carried high fees, and the broker hadn't managed them. He had advised her to make one bad decision after another. He hadn't looked out for her best interest. He hadn't protected her.

My mother never got to see the Chinese terracotta soldiers. More than two millennia ago, the thirteen-year-old emperor Qin Shi Huang ordered the construction of his own mausoleum, with thousands of life-size figures of warriors, horses, and chariots buried nearby. He hoped they would protect him for all time, advancing against any threat to his dominion. In 1974, farmers digging a well discovered a few of the figures, and archaeologists eventually unearthed the army. The soldiers, centuries in the dust, had not moved an inch.[1]

Only the emperor could tell us whether his men served their purpose, and he's not talking. But this I know: In today's world, legions of "advisors" promise lasting security to their clients, but very few of them come close to fulfilling that hope. If you are to enjoy the retirement of your dreams, you will need someone standing staunchly at your side. You will not need an army, but you certainly will need an advocate. You worked long and hard for what you have gained. Don't let it slip away.

REGRETS AND RESOLVE

There, at the Jersey Shore beach house that I once called home, I began sorting through the past. My mother and father bought that house in the early 1960s, and there they made their life together and raised their family. Both my parents were now gone, but it seemed I could still hear their voices. Their presence was all around me in those rooms.

---

1 "Tang dynasty," Wikipedia, https://en.wikipedia.org/wiki/Tang_dynasty.

My mom was an optimistic soul who only saw the good in people. I once met one of her former pupils who recalled being sent to the corner of the classroom for some childish transgression, thirty years earlier—and yet remembered the incident fondly. My mother had the knack of disciplining without punishing.

My father grew up in Atlantic City during its heyday; his parents operated a hotel and boarding house there. He joined the army during the Korean War, because he saw the value in getting a full GI Bill education for serving only eighteen months. He believed in rules. You didn't have to like them, and you could try to change them, but you should work within the system and use it to your advantage as best you could. That was his philosophy—somewhat cynical, but highly practical.

At the time of my mother's death, I had been working in the financial services industry for the better part of two decades. For much of my career, I had worked for some of the nation's most affluent families, yet I couldn't recall ever talking about money with my own parents. My father used to buy gold coins, and I would see him reading financial newsletters, but I never sat down with him and Mom to talk about their financial situation. Even after making my career in the industry, I never broached the subject with them.

"They must be doing okay," I told myself. If anything were wrong, surely they'd tell me. They only had one car (a Chevy), and they never took big trips or did much of anything extravagant. That is the way I grew up, so I figured that was just how things were with them.

Both had held down steady jobs, after all. My mother had her teacher's pension, and my father had a pension from his eighteen years as a New Jersey government worker. When they retired in the early 1990s pensions were not as generous as they became later in the decade during the big bull market, when many people imagined the good times might last forever.

I think my parents had to be very careful about their spending. With their pensions and Social Security benefits, they were getting by—but not much more than that. If my mother had lived, she would have been in a difficult financial situation within four or five years. She didn't have the reserves to deal with inflation and other pressures. She probably would have had to sell her house.

I wish I could say I stepped in and helped them make the right choices. Instead, I was upset with myself for having never talked about money with them.

I've found that such a lack of financial communication is common between parents and their children. Many people feel that money is one of those things you just don't talk about. It's private. They don't want even their own children to know the extent of their wealth. Affluent families may want their children to learn the value of hard work and initiative. Struggling families may feel embarrassed about mistakes they've made. In general, open communication increases the potential for thorough and efficient planning, through which both generations will benefit.

I regret that I didn't share with my parents what I knew about financial planning and investments. I should have asked them how they were doing, no matter how it might have seemed to me. You might think it unconscionable that my mother's advisor at the brokerage firm would be doing anything less than the best for a first-grade teacher. After all, aren't those large financial houses trying to present themselves as geniuses with vast resources at their command? They lure people in by telling them they will be in good hands. Often, though, they do not deliver on that promise—for a lot of reasons, not the least of which is that they are looking out for their own bottom line.

At that point in my life, I had already built and sold a business and was doing some consulting, but the pace of my career had slowed. I'm not good at doing nothing. When I finally recognized that my parents had struggled for years, I made a vow to myself: "I'm going to make sure this doesn't happen to other folks."

I come from a family of educators. Besides my mother, my grandmother and aunt were teachers and my sister became a college professor—and that's just to name a few. I decided to make education and advocacy the focus of a new phase in my career. I felt that it should be my mission to make a difference. I wanted to share my experience and expertise to help people avoid the kind of trap that ensnared my mom.

I founded my current company, TFG Wealth Management, in 2007—perfect timing, considering how many people would, within a few years, desperately need the kind of dedicated service and financial wisdom that I could offer them. I decided to provide wealth management services, which included financial planning, investment services, and more for people preparing to retire. I would be their advocate, telling them the truth about the financial system and how to deal with it. I recognized that a lot of people might run from the truth, but I also knew that nothing gets solved without openness and honesty.

I am the product of my upbringing and what I have learned and observed through the years, both personally and professionally. It has shaped me into who I am, and it is why I do what I do.

EDUCATION AND ADVOCACY

As I was beginning my new path at TFG Wealth Management, the wife and son of a veteran came to me with an astounding story. After being asked to leave a rehab facility when their Medicare benefits ran out, the director of the facility suggested that they apply for special veterans benefits and recommended a local attorney who could help them. The attorney had offered to help the family collect $20,000 a year in Veterans Affairs (VA) benefits for a $13,000 fee. They figured they didn't really have a choice, so they agreed. When the VA declined their application because of incomplete paperwork, the lawyer told them, "Sorry, I can't help you"—but he still kept their money.

I did a lot of research, consulted with the local congressional office, and figured out what to do. I soon saw the full extent of how often unscrupulous people take advantage of veterans. There was no need for them to pay anything to obtain a benefit that was rightfully theirs. They just needed to know how to apply.

The government allows only specially designated Veteran Service Officers to help with VA paperwork, so I became one. Most Veteran Service Officers have military experience, but I did not and was quite an unusual exception. Still, I took the tests and obtained the required sponsorship. I wanted to personally right this wrong.

I knew that my focus on education and advocacy would require frequent speaking engagements, but I'd never spoken in front of groups before. I realized that the more I did it, the better I would become at it. I started speaking at nursing homes and assisted living communities in the Philadelphia and New Jersey region at least once a week, explaining how to obtain veterans' benefits and deal with other concerns, all the while emphasizing that I was not out to sell anything. My advice was pro bono.

What I gained was confidence. If I was to be an educator, I had to develop the skills to educate. Likewise, I gained confidence and skill in writing by becoming financial editor for a local magazine and by posting blogs and articles on many financial websites hosted by Forbes, Fortune, Morningstar, newspapers, and others.

In my years working with veterans, I helped about three hundred families obtain an average of about $15,000 a year in VA benefits. Recently, the daughter of one of those veterans became a client of mine, telling me that she would always remember what I had done for her dad, who had recently passed away. I was more than happy to have helped. It angered me that veterans were not getting the respect that they deserved.

My clients often ask me whether I am a Democrat or Republican, a conservative or liberal. I tell them that I am their advocate no matter who is in office. I often think of my father and his advice to work within the system, changing what we can but always using it to our best advantage. I work with the existing policies and rules to do what is best for those I serve.

NEVER A DOUBT

I did consider a military career, in keeping with family tradition. Members of my family served in the Civil War and in both world wars—some with high rank. It was that legacy, in part, that led me to apply to Annapolis after high school. And for a young man who also loved to row crew, Annapolis certainly was the place to go. But then I was offered a nearly full academic scholarship and early admission to Columbia University, and to accept the scholarship I had to withdraw all my applications to other institutions, including Yale and Virginia. I could not pass up such an opportunity.

At Columbia, I studied computer engineering, a new major in the early 1980s. My father had advised me, with good reason, that computers were the future. I accepted and respected his practical approach. There was only one problem. I discovered that I hated computers. I hated programming. Still, I graduated and accepted a job at Burroughs Corporation, which later became Unisys.

Looking for a way to combine what I did for a living with my desire to help people, I applied to the University of Pennsylvania to study nonprofit management and finance. I was accepted on a full scholarship and earned my degree in eighteen months.

While there, I met G. Edward DeSeve, my finance professor. Ed was prominent in the financial services industry and in government. When I was about to graduate, Ed told me, "I have a job for you when you graduate," and he asked me to help launch the Pennsylvania Economic Development Financing Authority. I started that agency from scratch, and after a year I took a position closer to Philadelphia, at the old-line brokerage W.H. Newbold's Son & Co., where Ed was president of the public finance unit. Newbold's employed some of the most highly experienced investment advisors in the region.

Later, when Newbold's was selling off some of its inventory, I began contacting local wealthy families, looking for buyers. That's when I met the Rosenwalds, members of the Forbes 400[2] whose initial fortune came from their part ownership of Sears, Roebuck & Co. They didn't want to buy anything I was selling, but they did offer to hire me to start their own trust company and mutual fund company. In doing so, I met other wealthy families around the country who had relationships with the Rosenwalds. The family was pleased with my work, but after several years they changed direction and began selling off what we had built.

After that, I started a firm that helped small- and medium-size businesses with their pension and 401(k) accounts, profit sharing, and benefits plans. We became their outsourced human resources department, helping with a range of employee issues. By 2001, I had sold that firm and was working as a consultant. It was about that time that my father died, and my mother's death several years later precipitated the founding of my current company.

So many people hold themselves back with their preconceived notions about what they cannot do. I believe that we can all achieve our dreams if we really want to.

Today, when I ask couples about their vision for the future, I often hear comments such as "We just don't have enough money to do that," or "We just have to accept that we won't be traveling much." I ask them to hold off on the negativity and just tell me what they want their retirement to look like. Even if they can't buy a Bentley, I still need to hear what they want to accomplish—then, together, we can look for the way to make it happen.

I founded TFG Wealth Management with a mission not just to educate folks about the financial system but also to help them make their retirement vision a reality.

A Word of Caution

During speaking engagements, I sometimes begin by displaying a crystal ball. I acquired one long ago while accompanying my wife on a business trip to Puerto Vallarta, Mexico. While she was busy, I poked around town and saw this sparkling clear orb and purchased it for the equivalent of five dollars. I have kept it ever since.

Let me assure you: The crystal ball doesn't work. It doesn't predict the future. In fact, it serves to remind me—and my audiences—that nobody can do that. I still find it necessary to point that out. As I look out on the faces in the audience, I know that many of the attendees are wondering two things: Where will the market be heading in the next six months? And what is the single best investment where they can put their money?

I answer the first question by pointing to my crystal ball. "Anybody who tells you that they know where the market is going in the next six months is basically full of it," I explain. "They're trying to sell you something. So far, this crystal ball hasn't done anything but sit there and look pretty."

To answer that second question, I will either show a picture of a silver bullet, and in some cases I will pull out a replica of a silver bullet. "I know that some of you are looking to discover that next great investment. You want to be at the front of the line for the next Google or the next Apple. Sorry, but nobody knows that for sure, and if they did, they wouldn't be telling you. They would invest every dime they have, rake in a fortune, and go off to their own private island in the Caribbean. And they wouldn't particularly want to invite you or me along for the ride."

In other words, there is no silver bullet, and you won't find the answers shimmering within some crystal ball. Success isn't about identifying the next hot product or murmuring "abracadabra."

You find success when you understand how the financial system truly operates, so that nobody takes advantage of you. Then you make your money work for you through some basic but little-known strategies that help you grow your wealth efficiently and effectively.

In fact, you might want to think about crystal balls with the same sort of suspicion that the Houston airport security officers displayed when they saw my new acquisition shining in my suitcase as we returned home from Mexico. It inspired them to tear my luggage apart. I can only imagine the commotion if they had found a silver bullet, too.

GETTING THE RIGHT ADVICE

I wrote *this book* for you to go over the important financial issues everyone must consider to have a successful retirement. All the things I wish I had shared with my mom so she would have been better prepared for retirement. Along the journey to and through retirement, you will meet many people who are eager to give you advice about what to do with your money and how to live your life. So how do you know whose advice to take?

Here are the **three questions** you should ask yourself before deciding who to listen to.

QUESTION 1: WHAT KIND OF ADVICE DO YOU NEED?

If you are reading this book, you have probably decided you need some extra advice about how to prepare for retirement. One of the biggest and most common mistakes I see is that people skip a very important step in the process of choosing an advisor: They don't take the time to determine what kind of advice they need. Typically, they will just look for someone with the next great investment strategy; or maybe they believe that all advisors are the same, so it doesn't really matter. I am here to tell you that those people are dead wrong.

Throughout this book, I will discuss the many different issues that you will face as you journey to and through your retirement. These will include issues like coping with inflation, dealing with market volatility, generating income, making your money last, and dealing with taxes, health care costs, and estate issues. It is these issues that will have a greater impact on your future financial security than which asset allocation you choose. Because there are no silver bullets, and crystal balls can't predict the future, you need to determine which of these issues are most important to you and which will have the most impact—in a positive *and* negative way—on your financial security.

Everyone is different and unique. While the list of concerns is the same for everyone, how they impact each person's financial security can be very different. This is why the first step I take with anyone who comes in to meet with me is to determine which of these issues are most important to focus on and which can be pushed off on the side, because they will not significantly impact that person's financial future.

QUESTION 2: WHAT KIND OF ADVISOR DO YOU NEED?

To most of you reading this book, this question may not make a lot of sense, because you probably think all advisors are the same. The fact is that there are many different kinds of advisors who provide very different kinds of advice, and the advice they will give you can be held to very different standards.

In a later section of the book, I will discuss the difference between an *investment consultant* and a *wealth manager*, the two general categories of services provided by advisors. I will also discuss the difference between the *fiduciary* standard of care and the *suitability* standard of care, which are the two legal standards used to measure the quality of the advice given by financial professionals.

QUESTION 3: WHAT TYPE OF PLANS AND STRATEGIES DO YOU NEED?

One thing is certain: Everyone needs a plan. Some plans will be more complicated than others, but without a plan—a road map—there is no way to be certain you will reach your destination. There are many types of plans, which serve very different purposes:

- basic financial plan
- income plan
- investment plan
- tax plan
- health care and custodial care plan
- estate plan

Each of these plans addresses a different concern you will face during your retirement. If you put them all together, you have what I call a *Wealth Strategy*.

Most families I meet do not have any type of plan or strategy for their future. If they do, it's usually a financial plan put together years before and never reviewed, let alone changed, as they got closer to retirement. A few may have an investment strategy that spells out how their money should be invested or allocated between different asset classes. The investment strategy was almost always created with no consideration for their real retirement needs.

When I worked for very wealthy individuals and families, I learned that it takes much more than just a basic budget, financial plan, or even an investment strategy to truly be successful in your financial life. For that, you need a Wealth Strategy.

I firmly believe that a Wealth Strategy is not just for the super wealthy—everyone deserves one so that they too can be successful during retirement. It's another one of the reasons I wrote this book. A Wealth Strategy anticipates problems before they happen, provides answers to questions beyond just what asset allocation you should use, and always keeps you on track.

Throughout the chapters of this book, I will take you on a journey to build your own retirement Wealth Strategy. Each chapter is a step on the path toward making your vision of retirement a reality.

Decide for yourself which areas of your Wealth Strategy are important, find the right advisor, and get started on your journey to a happy and financially secure retirement.

At the end of this book, you will find a checklist of the steps along this journey. This will tell you what you need to do to create your Wealth Strategy.

Chapter 1

"AM I ON THE RIGHT PATH?"

Do you have a Wealth Strategy for the future?

When approaching retirement, most folks have more questions than answers. Will my money last? Have I prepared properly? Do I have the right investments? This fear can often lead to making poor decisions about your future and creating more problems than they solve. You must remove this fear of the unknown before you can have a successful retirement.

" I quit my job!" the successful executive exclaimed. I was concerned, for a moment, but her face was beaming—I could not help but smile broadly, too. This was success.

Paula, who was in her late fifties, had grown exasperated with her high-pressure position at a Fortune 50 firm. Thirty years of stress had left her feeling miserable, though she was making over $200,000 a year.

"Look, I can't take it anymore," Paula had told me at our first meeting. "I need to get out of there. This is not what I want to do with my life." Her real dream, she told me, was to work at an amusement park. "I love kids," she said. She imagined herself helping to manage a food concession. She wanted to be around happy people who were having fun. She wanted to do her job and then go home. It was clear she was dying inside as the years passed and the dream still seemed a mirage.

Paula's previous advisor had told her that she had to keep her executive job, because she and her husband didn't have enough money to allow her to essentially retire, though their investments at the time were approaching a million dollars. He told her that she could not just chuck it all for some low-paying job.

"He warned me that we probably would have to sell our house, and our kids might not be able to finish their education." Paula and her husband had two children in college. "He gave me every reason under the sun why I should just keep plugging away at this job I hate." She looked deflated. I thought she might cry.

At that first meeting, Paula and I took some time to explore the possibilities, though she hadn't yet hired me. "I don't know just yet whether you can retire," I told her, "but my job is to figure out if you can, and how. I can tell you what you would need to do to make it happen, and you may like it or you may not. That's for you to decide. I'm here to help you understand how it all works together."

That is a role I often play. I help you refine your vision. I help you get a clear picture of where you are today and where you want to go. Then, together, we work up a Wealth Strategy to get there. We make sure you find the right path and stay on it. Together, we make your vision of retirement a reality.

Paula and I developed a preliminary strategy for how she might realize her vision. I did an analysis, and at our second meeting I told her the results: "Paula, you clearly could do this, but here's what has to happen. First, your husband has to agree that he will work until he is sixty-six." She told me that was indeed his intention, and that his job was stable.

"Great," I said, "so if you can make at least $20,000 a year from your job at the park, add that to the Social Security benefits, and make a 4.5 percent return with your investments, then your dream is possible." It would call for close monitoring to make sure they stayed on track, but it certainly was possible for her to step out of the executive swirl and still maintain her desired lifestyle. "Think about it," I told her, "and make sure to talk it over carefully with your husband."

The next time I saw her, Paula was a different woman as she stepped lightly into my office and announced what she had done. "Mark," she said, "I quit my job, and I am ready to implement our plan."

I hadn't expected such swift action, and I certainly don't recommend impulsive decisions. "Paula, we haven't even implemented your plan," I cautioned, but she had glimpsed her path to real success, and she was eager to get on it.

"No problem," she said. "I can see how it works. I understand what you're going to do, and I believe in it. Let's get going!" She was not acting impulsively. I could tell that she was acting confidently, finally able to see her way.

Paula proceeded to get her job at the park, and then she found another dream: She went back to college. Today, she works with young people as an instructor at a local college. She has redirected her life into new activities—ones that matter to her.

REALIZING YOUR RETIREMENT VISION

The stated mission of my firm is to *help families realize their vision of retirement*. Yes, we manage money, and we help with estate matters and all the other elements of a Wealth Strategy, but it all comes down to pursuing the dream—your dream!

Most advisors are investment consultants. They try to figure out your risk tolerance and then implement investments accordingly. But risk is a double-edged sword. It could help you, or it could hurt you. The more risk you take, the more money you might make—and the more you might lose. But what investment consultants don't do is take the time to understand why. Why have you saved your money for the last twenty or thirty years? Why have you sacrificed to make sure you have the nest egg you need for retirement?

That is why effective wealth management requires much more than asking how much risk you feel you could tolerate. The plan and the process must be right for you, and they can't be right for you unless they advance your vision of retirement.

It's not unusual for advisors to tell people they cannot have their dream. That's because when families are pursuing a dream, they very well might be spending some of the money that the advisor would otherwise manage. It's a sad truth in the financial industry. By contrast, I help people attain their desired lifestyle. I help them with the pursuit of happiness.

Financial advisors make money on their clients' money. It's that simple. The less money clients have available to manage, the less money advisors can make. Advisors make more money when they manage more of it. I believe that advisors should not be motivated that way. My job is to help you achieve your vision for the future. It is a different approach that might not seem the most lucrative of business models, but I've found that the more you give, the more you get. The more I can do to help people, the more successful I will be.

Every month, my company sees hundreds of thousands of dollars that we manage go out the door in distributions. It is the nature of business for retirement specialists—and every day we also see families realize their dreams. Advisors who just help you grow your money during the accumulation years do not experience that outflow. They don't understand what it takes to make sure your money is there when you need it. This all means retirement specialists like me must be even better at what we do. You deserve to make good use of the money you worked so hard to save.

CHANGING PERSPECTIVES

In my years as a wealth manager, I have often heard variations of a question that reflects a deep fear: "Am I going to have enough?" You may also be wondering that. No matter how much money you have, you may still harbor a deep concern about whether you have done the right things to set yourself up for the rest of your life.

"We have nothing to fear but fear itself," Franklin Delano Roosevelt famously declared during the Great Depression. A lack of understanding leads people astray, sometimes causing them to make quick decisions that worsen their situation. Practical, commonsense planning is the solution. Once you understand how your money works and what it is supposed to do—once you fully grasp the nature of the risks you face—your fears tend to disappear. When you can see the path clearly leading to your destination, you feel ready to move forward. There are risks at every turn of that path, and in this book, we will explore a variety of them. By carefully managing risk, you ensure that your money will last. I believe the correct approach is to reduce risk as much as you reasonably can. The less risk you must take, the more likely your money will see you through your lifetime.

Making the right decisions requires working with an advisor willing to spend the time to counsel and educate you. Occasionally, people will ask me whether I can make them rich if they hand over all their money. Those who would say that simply do not understand their money. It is likely that nobody has ever explained to them the nature of each of their investments and what they can expect in up markets and down markets. Nobody has pointed out to them how investment strategies must change as one gets closer to retirement.

Retirement is a new phase of life. Your years of accumulation are ending. It is a time for a greater focus on protection. Failure to adjust to that reality can jeopardize your retirement portfolio. You need to learn what works and to work with someone who will help you to learn.

When you were younger and saving for retirement, the focus of your plan was fairly simple. You might have figured that if you put away, say, $10,000 or $20,000 a year, the markets over the long haul likely would boost your investments to the point where you would have enough to reasonably retire by a particular date.

As you approach that date, however, you find that the rules have changed. For one thing, you can't say for sure how long your money will need to last, because it is hard to predict how long you will last. You might live a few years, or you might live for thirty years. Your spouse might die before you or long outlive you. Regardless, when those paychecks end, you will need to create your own paychecks.

This is an entirely different perspective. When you were younger, growth was the priority for your portfolio. Now, you need to preserve your savings while using it to produce an income to support your lifestyle. You still need growth, but it is not the biggest concern. Your perspectives are—or should be—changing dramatically.

YOUR WEALTH STRATEGY

Every day I meet with people who wonder whether they are on the right path. What they need, I tell them, is a Wealth Strategy. There is an investment strategy, a tax strategy, an income strategy, and an estate strategy; wealth comes from employing a combination of all of those. Leave one out, and financial security is in danger.

As you flip through these pages, you might choose to start with a chapter dealing with whatever concerns you most at the moment. Many people have a pressing problem when they come in to see me. Perhaps they are grappling with a tax or estate predicament, or they may just be seeking guidance on how to structure their pension or when to begin taking their Social Security benefit. First we deal with your most pressing problems then we broaden the discussions, exploring the many layers of financial planning. And that is how I've written this book—although I do recommend you read it cover to cover, because all those elements interconnect and overlap.

If you are thinking about retirement, you need an overall strategy, and that calls for starting with the right mind-set. Have you identified the purpose of your wealth? Until you do so, your money is not serving you—you are serving it. Finding that purpose is where you need to start, and that is where we start in this book. Only by getting to know you and understanding your vision can I help you get all the pieces in place to reach it.

Different things become more important as time passes. In general, retirees first look outward, then inward, and then into the future. For the first five years or so, they take their dream trips and pursue other pent-up desires, then they focus on family and friends and self-development, and then they look to their legacy. People evolve. Looking back, it feels as if you were a different person at age thirty. Likewise, you're a different person at seventy, or eighty, or ninety.

Each of us has unique retirement dreams. We each have our own idea of what we want our money to do for us. Therefore, our approach should and will differ from family to family. You and your neighbor will deal differently with such matters as inflation, cash flow, market volatility, health care issues, and estate matters. Your Wealth Strategy must be tailored to your circumstances and goals. The cookie-cutter approach doesn't work.

True wealth will bring a sense of freedom. Wealthy people are those who can do what they choose to do, not what they have to do. Retirement is not necessarily the time when you stop working. You very well may decide that you want to work, but you do not have to work if you are truly retired. It is more than money that makes you rich. Having money gives you more choices, but you are not rich until you make the choices that bring purpose to your life. I believe that my client Paula became a wealthy retiree on the day that she decided to take a job at the amusement park.

That is why I have no easy answer when people start out by asking me, as they so often do, where they should put their money or what the hot investment of the moment is. Those decisions will depend on what is going on in their lives. If I do my job right, the investment strategy will be the easiest thing that we do. If we discover together the issues and risks that are involved and why it all matters, it should soon become obvious which investments will make the most sense. The hard part is what we do up front. The details then tend to fall into place.

RETIREMENT IS A PROCESS, NOT AN EVENT

Retirement isn't just a date you mark on the calendar. It should begin long before the retirement party and continue to develop for a lifetime. It starts with an assessment of your financial picture: If nothing were to change in it, would that be acceptable? The process continues by defining and refining life goals: Are your assets sufficient to get to the desired destination? If not, what needs to be done?

Many people do not start that process or get stalled, because they think they need exact answers. That can be an impossible expectation. Each step involves unknowns. We cannot be certain about taxes, inflation, or longevity, for example.

In his book *The 80% Approach*, Dan Sullivan, founder of the Strategic Coach program, develops what he calls a transformative way to eliminate the paralysis of perfectionism and procrastination. If you are 80 percent sure of the answers at each step, he says, then keep going.

But it doesn't stop there. We must work together to effectively deal with all the risks. We can make adjustments along the way, revisiting the customized Wealth Strategy—your Wealth Strategy—regularly and reviewing any of the assumptions on which it's built. We deal with each uncertainty as it arises. That's how we stay on track. Step by step, we can get ever closer to that elusive perfection—but if you expect it at the gate, it will be hard to get started.

Worrying over past mistakes can also halt progress. You cannot change the past. Instead, you should work to understand the present and plan for the future. Everyone has made both good and bad financial decisions. But you can only make better decisions by developing strategies based on a greater understanding of risks and rewards. Armed with new insight, you can move forward. Think of retirement as a process—not an event.

ARE WE A GOOD FIT?

Recently I helped a couple assess their resources and their goals, and we determined that they needed a conservative 3.5 percent return (in addition to accounting for inflation) in order to retire to their satisfaction. They were cautious by nature, and that was all the growth they needed to meet their expectations for the rest of their days.

If my goal had just been to see that they beat the market, I would have suggested they put all their money into equities and managed their portfolio as best I could. That would have put them at risk of experiencing another year like 2008 and I would have had to say to them, even if their investments were ahead of the market, "I'm sorry, but no retirement for you." That kind of risk was not their idea of a carefree retirement. Instead, I suggested they put half their money into CDs to earn a few percent guaranteed. I made nothing from those transactions. And then we put the rest of their money into large-cap equities and bonds to boost their returns to provide them with a secure and comfortable future.

I like to work with people who want to make the most of their retirement and get the most out of life, however they define it. I don't want to be viewed as just an order taker who sets up the investments. Rather, I prefer to work with people who want a relationship with their advisor. We can be friends, but the professional relationship comes first.

"I've been sitting down every year with my advisor for a long time," folks often tell me, "and he asks me about my family and tells me about his family, but we never seem to talk about my money or about where we are with my plan." I assure them that will not be the case with me. Yes, we will take time to catch up and get to know each other, but the primary focus will be on understanding what's going on with their money. They will leave knowing how their Wealth Strategy is doing.

I appreciate people who are actively engaged in their financial affairs and who seem interested in more than whether I can help them make as much money as possible. What I do goes well beyond the role of investment consultant. I do help with the investments, of course, but that isn't my sole purpose. If you just want to beat the market, this book is not for you, and we wouldn't be a good fit.

Yes, you will want strong investments with a good return, but your overall strategy must be designed so that only a reasonable proportion of your money is exposed to market risk. A prevailing misconception is that the market is the measure of success or failure, and if you do better than the market, you are a winner. Remember the two rules of investing attributed to Warren Buffett: 1) never lose money; and 2) never forget the first rule. If all your money is in the market, which is down 30 percent, but your portfolio is only down 25 percent, you are beating the market—but are you doing well?

Any advisor who would call that success is just looking for an easy out. Will that attitude pave the way to your dreams? Will you feel good about that? What you should feel good about is a Wealth Strategy that allows you to live your chosen lifestyle and to do the things you want to do.

"YES, YOU CAN RETIRE."

I love the days when I can tell a couple that all is well and they can retire. Sometimes it is the culmination of years of planning as we structured strategies to meet their goals. And then the day comes when we are reviewing their finances, and either husband or wife looks up and asks, "So does this mean the time has come?" It is my joy when I can respond: "Absolutely, you are right on track. Yes, you can retire."

I work with people from many walks of life who have a wide range of incomes and savings. Some have as little as $250,000 when they come in, and some have tens of millions of dollars. I'll meet with anyone I can truly help. I don't start out asking you how much money you have, as if to turn you away. If I can be of service, we will work together. If I cannot—if you are doing just fine, for example, and I could not significantly improve your situation—then I'll say so.

My clients include business owners, teachers, clergy, law enforcement officers, farmers, and corporate executives. I have clients who are mushroom growers from Chester County and Philadelphia police officers. I serve FBI agents and US Marshals. I serve priests and ministers and rabbis. I serve nurses and doctors.

My clients range in age from their late forties to their nineties, although most first come to me when they are between fifty and sixty-five. They are looking forward to retiring or are already beginning that transition. Many of them were with other advisors for a decade or two. They have come to understand that they need a different kind of advice in this time of life.

Often, people who think they have a financial plan in place have just been given a tool that was designed to sell a product. Once the salesperson gets a commission, the buyer never opens the financial plan again. Others haven't even thought about how they will achieve their goals. They carefully plan their careers and vacations, and they save up for their big purchases, but for some reason they don't take the time to contemplate how life will change on the day they retire. Life gets in the way, as they dash from here to there, and sometimes they fear that planning will confirm their fear that they are in financial trouble. Nonetheless, the day of retirement will come.

Some folks are naturally more inclined to engage in detailed planning. I know one couple who lay out their year in January, deciding specifically how much money they will need and how much they will spend. They figure out exactly what they will do and how they will do it. Others tend to be, let's say, more casual.

I believe it is a financial advisor's job to keep you on course, not just manage your investments to a certain level of risk tolerance. If you go off course, it is my duty to call you in for a hard conversation and warn you that you risk losing sight of your destination, even though you might not feel the financial pain for a while. You might presume you have plenty, but a good financial professional will help you to see dire consequences of today's decisions that are, perhaps, a decade down the road. It is your money to do with as you wish, of course, but if you have hired me to help you, then I will hold you accountable.

As you venture into the chapters ahead, let me ask you this essential and central question: If you have a financial plan, when was the last time you looked at it? When was the last time you updated it? And if you do not have a plan, why not? Your financial future is at stake. It's time to take action. If you want to make smarter decisions with your money to help secure a rewarding retirement, read on.

QUESTIONS TO CONSIDER

- ⦿ What is my Wealth Strategy for the future?
- ⦿ Am I making decisions out of fear or from the confidence of knowing where I am heading?
- ⦿ Who can I depend on for advice that serves my interests?
- ⦿ How will I know if I get off course during retirement?

Chapter 2

THE NEW YOU

What is your vision of retirement?

Retirement is an exciting new phase of life, full of opportunities. But it can also be troubling—financially and emotionally. You have a lot more time to enjoy life, but your portfolio has a lot less time to recover from mistakes. You must prepare for the transition. Are you ready for the challenge?

As I reviewed Bob and Mary's income sources, I noticed that Mary was earning three or four hundred dollars a week taking care of children. I asked her to tell me more about the job: Was she working at a daycare? Who were these children?

"My grandkids," she said.

By day, she is the babysitter. At night, she's Grandma. She made it clear to her daughter that she's happy to watch the grandkids anytime in the evenings, but during the daytime, she will charge for child care.

Why? Because Mary has found herself to be busier than ever in retirement, with so many things she wants to do and accomplish. Those morning and afternoon hours are in high demand. Sure, she loves the grandkids every bit as much when she sees them by the light of day, but she also feels she should be compensated for the time that is taken away from the other things she loves to do. You see, Bob's and her vision of their retirement is to take classes, meet friends, run errands, and enjoy their time as a couple.

It was an unusual arrangement but quite an understandable one. Bob and Mary set a boundary. They would take care of the grandkids, but they would also take care of themselves. People work hard for years to get to retirement. They make many sacrifices. They postpone many of the things they have long wanted to do.

You may recall the movie *The Bucket List*, starring Jack Nicholson and Morgan Freeman as two men whose days have been numbered by illness. Before they "kick the bucket," they set out together on a series of adventures to experience their lifelong dreams. Many of today's retirees have their own bucket lists, although generally they are in better health than people their age have ever been. Especially in the first few years of retirement, they focus on that list, though it may not be a formal one. They want to take the trips they dreamed of and pursue the hobbies and other activities they have put off for so long.

A NEW WORLD

The realities of retirement catch some people by surprise. What they imagined is not what they are experiencing. I conduct a six-hour class on retirement planning. Those attending often expect that the market and investments will be top on the agenda. Instead, I focus the first part of the class on what they are going to do with all that time on their hands. Do they have a hobby? Have they thought about how they will be filling their days? For a happy retirement, it is essential to get a grip on how you will spend your time.

My wife, who is a corporate executive, is younger than me but will retire first. A few years ago, she started taking art classes, joined a fitness program, and began playing tennis a few days a week. She saw that retirement was on her horizon and recognized the need to further develop her interests and expand her activities to ease the transition into retirement. As for me, I intend to continue operating my business for quite some time. I like what I do.

After years on the job, you don't want to wake up one Monday morning with the disturbing realization that you have nowhere to go. You need to prepare yourself mentally, as well as financially, for retirement. With years of good living still to come and forty or more additional hours a week at your disposal, what will you do to make that time meaningful? You won't just be strolling on the beach or rocking on the porch for forty hours a week. These days, most retirees are leaving jobs that are not as labor-intensive as they were in generations past. Hard physical work has not taken its toll on their bodies, and they are fit and full of energy.

I have clients who travel the country by motorcycle. When I call to discuss some matter, they might be cruising through Death Valley or over the salt flats of Utah (if I can reach them at all). Another gentleman began competing in triathlons after he retired. Others have become deeply involved in renovating their houses. They take pride in their homes and their communities and become more involved in local affairs. Others pack up and relocate to some dream location.

The families I work with are generally in good financial shape, but I do understand that many people struggle. Some need to return to work to pay the bills, often accepting jobs for a fraction of the pay they once commanded. Retirement shouldn't be a distressing time, and yet for many it is—if not financially, then emotionally. The transition into this phase of life can be stressful.

Many people have long found much of their identity in the workplace. They may feel empty inside once they leave it. They miss their friends and associates. Some return to work not so much for financial reasons but rather to regain the feeling that they are contributing. They may become consultants or mentors to younger people in their profession. Others volunteer at a nonprofit or serve on a board. Some run for political office.

Couples need to take care that the inherent stresses of this change in life do not rock their marriage. Retirement can lead to a lot more togetherness, for better and for worse. Smart couples recognize that each still needs a degree of independence, with separate activities that reflect their interests.

A few years ago, I received a call from a couple looking for some help planning for their retirement. Charlotte stayed at home and took care of the house while Hank, who was in his early seventies, went off to work every day. I assumed they had called me because Hank was planning to retire. So when I showed up at their house for a review, I was so proud of the fact that Hank could retire immediately that I couldn't help but start our meeting by telling Hank and Charlotte the good news.

To my surprise, Charlotte scowled. "No! He's not retiring. I don't want him around the house!" Hank looked taken aback, for just a moment, but then a smile crept over his face.

Hank worked several more years at his engineering job, finally retiring at age seventy-eight. Today he teaches youngsters at his church. He keeps busy. He and Charlotte were wise enough to know that neither of them would be happy just hanging around the house all day. They made sure they had a regular routine.

It can take some time to get in the groove of retirement. Any major change in life requires adjustment, such as when you go off to college, when you get married, or when you have children. The key is to know what to expect financially, socially, and emotionally. Retirement is a new world. It is exciting, certainly, and filled with opportunities, but it can be troubling as well. You need to prepare for the challenges.

THE MEASURE OF TIME

When we are young, we tend to be preoccupied with starting a family, buying a house, and saving for our children's college expenses while perhaps paying off our own tuition and dealing with an increasing debt load. Then we focus on advancing in our careers and getting promotions and raises. The years seem to stretch ahead without end.

Younger people, as they attend to life's preoccupations, often pay little attention to retirement until all their children have launched out on their own. That's when they awaken to this next big challenge. Unfortunately, if they have done absolutely no retirement planning up to that point, they may be in trouble. It is hard to save enough if you don't start until you are in your fifties.

As retirement approaches, time is no longer your ally. Mistakes made as you get closer to retirement and while you are retired are often magnified, because you don't have time to recover. While you could previously rely on compounding—a powerful investment principle—to help grow your wealth over decades, now you need to not only continue to grow your money but also to generate income to support your lifestyle.

As retirement nears, what I see the most is that the average person will shift their investments from a more aggressive portfolio to a more conservative one and think they have properly prepared for retirement. While repositioning your investments is a good start, it is only the beginning of proper retirement planning. Often missing are all the other aspects of a Wealth Strategy you will need to survive and thrive in retirement. These aspects include preparing for the toll taxes and inflation will take on your retirement savings, for emergencies that might sap your savings, and for a prolonged illness or a crippling lawsuit. How will your money generate income efficiently and effectively in retirement? How will your estate plan properly and efficiently leave your wealth to your spouse, children, grandchildren, and other heirs? These issues (and many more) are key components to a good Wealth Strategy.

In my speaking engagements, I sometimes bring out a tape measure and ask someone in the audience to stretch out the tape and put a thumb on his or her age. A sixty-two-year-old, for example, would stop at sixty-two inches. "Now, how long do you expect to live?" I ask, and the answer generally is about eighty-five or ninety. I then have them stretch the tape measure out until they reach the ninety-inch mark.

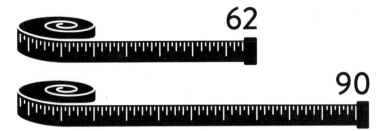

The demonstration helps people to visualize the timeline of their lives. They see how far they have come, and they see proportionately how far they have to go. It helps folks understand why they need to be more protective of their money. With time growing shorter, they can't afford mistakes anymore. As you look at your own timeline, ask yourself how you measure up. Have you taken the steps to ensure you will be all right as you face whatever life could bring your way?

CHANGE IN STRATEGIES

As you get older, you will need to adopt very different kinds of strategies from the ones you used to manage your money while accumulating it—strategies that protect and preserve your money, generate income, and grow your nest egg along the way. Because if you hold on to those earlier strategies and fail to adjust, you put your retirement at serious risk.

This does not mean that you should run scared. If all of your money goes into a bank account paying a pittance in interest, you will lose ground to inflation—hardly a sign of wise wealth management. If all your money goes into the stock market and we experience another 2008-type crash, how will you survive? This is why a Wealth Strategy—not just an investment strategy—is so important.

You see, preserving money and generating income require an entirely different discipline than saving and growing your money.

When you were working and getting those yearly raises, you probably didn't think so much about inflation. Now, unless you can give yourself a raise every year during retirement, you face the prospect of cutting back on your lifestyle as inflation erodes your resources. Inflation has changed from an abstraction to an important consideration when planning for retirement.

When you were working, you told yourself that the more money you put into your 401(k) plan, the more you were saving in taxes. What you didn't realize is that you were creating a tax nightmare that will destroy your retirement plan due to government rules and regulations, like required minimum distributions when you turn seventy-and-a-half.

When you were working and your investments went down, you could just buy more. If your investments take a turn for the worse while you are in retirement, what is your plan to generate income without compounding your losses.

When you were working, you probably maintained life insurance and disability insurance so that, in case your spouse died suddenly or became disabled, you could still pay your bills, make the mortgage, and put your kids through school. You prepared for the unexpected.

What you may not realize is that you also need to prepare for the sudden death or disability of your spouse during retirement. The reason for this is pretty straightforward, but most advisors and planners don't discuss this with their clients, let alone plan for this.

When your spouse passes away during retirement, you will lose part of your Social Security benefits, and your taxes could go up 20 to 30 percent. This could result in your income being cut in half from higher taxes and less Social Security income. Have you planned for how you are going to make up the loss of one Social Security benefit or pay the higher taxes owed because you are filing as a single taxpayer and not a joint taxpayer? Even worse, if one of you becomes ill, you could be facing hundreds of thousands of dollars for medical, custodial, and nursing care costs.

When you no longer are working, your money is more vulnerable. If something unexpected comes up and you need to dip into your retirement savings, it may not be possible to ever replace the extra money you needed to spend.

These are just a few of the new issues and concerns you will be facing for the next twenty or thirty years.

You aren't alone. I've worked with countless people just like you on their retirement journeys. I understand the adjustments they face, financially and otherwise. I know what they are going through. Their circumstances differ, sometimes dramatically, but the path of life is similar. The themes are the same. A good financial advisor who is working strictly on your behalf can help you sort it all out.

The highly affluent families I worked with earlier in my career understood how hard it was to create their wealth and how important it is to protect it. Like people nearing retirement, those families were no longer intent on growing their money as much as possible. Their concerns had refocused on making sure that they didn't lose all that the family had gained. They had made it, and they were managing their wealth to make sure that it served their purposes and goals. They understood the need for a Wealth Strategy—not just an investment strategy.

When you have gotten to the point where you can retire, you have made it. And you will want to keep it that way, which is why you need more than just an asset allocation plan—a Wealth Strategy that will protect your retirement from everything life has to throw at you.

QUESTIONS TO CONSIDER

- What is your vision for retirement?
- Have you considered how you will fill your retirement hours?
- Outside the workplace, how will you maintain the feeling that you are contributing?
- Do you intend to work or consult part time? Are you interested in volunteer work?
- Have you and your spouse talked about how you will adjust to retirement?
- Have you planned for the worse while hoping for the best in retirement?
- In what ways do you plan to change your investment strategies for this phase of life?

Chapter 3

YOUR RETIREMENT
& YOUR MONEY

Where are you going?

The numbers shouldn't come first in retirement planning. You need to get to the heart of the matter: What do you want out of life? You must define your destination first, and then we can work out the numbers to get there. Why did you set aside all that money? It's high time to define what matters most to you.

---

t is always exciting when I first meet with a couple. This is where it all gets started. After a few minutes of introduction, the next thing that usually happens is a pile of papers is pushed across the table. It may include bank and brokerage statements, a tax return, wills and trusts, and maybe an insurance or annuity policy. This is followed by "So how are we doing?" or "Do we have enough money to retire?"

My response is to carefully move all those papers off to one side and say, "We'll get to that in a minute, but first I need to get to know about you."

When developing a Wealth Strategy, the best place to start is not with your investments. It has to start with you. What are your values? What does money mean to you? What is all that money that you saved over the last thirty years going to do for you, for your spouse, for your family?

Many who walk through my door frankly haven't figured that out yet. I've found that a good place for them to start is to take a long look at where they came from and how they developed their attitude toward money.

EARLY EXPERIENCE WITH MONEY

I didn't grow up in a wealthy family. Our house in Margate, two towns down the shore from Atlantic City on Absecon Island, was on a twenty-five-by-seventy-five-foot lot. My parents had an air conditioner in their bedroom, and there was one in the dining room, so on simmering summer nights, I slept on my orange sleeping bag under the dining room table. Our dog kept me company. Nobody could step on us there.

If I wanted anything, I had to earn it. At age eleven, I started delivering the Philadelphia Bulletin, the afternoon paper. It was a start, but my real goal was to work my way up to delivering the local Atlantic City Press. After about a year, I finally got my route. The Press came out at 4 a.m. and had to be delivered by 7, so I got up daily well before dawn.

In Atlantic City in the summer, everyone worked on the boardwalk, at a hotel or restaurant. When I was fourteen, my father drove me to the inlet by the Steel Pier and dropped me off. It was about a dozen miles up the boardwalk. "Here's the deal," he said. "You start walking home, and look for a job all along the way. When you get one, give me a call. I'll come and pick you up."

I applied all along the boardwalk, and I finally got a lifeguard job at one of the motels. I called my dad: "Hey, I got a job! Come get me." As expected, he told me to take the bus. My father believed in being very self-reliant.

After a few weeks, my father decided I wasn't working enough. "I've found another job for you," he told me. It was as a bus boy at Mary's Restaurant on Tennessee Ave., where he stopped for breakfast across the street from his office. "You can work there for a couple of hours before going to your lifeguard job. Then you can come back and bus tables at dinner time."

Later I worked my way through college at a five-star restaurant where, even in 1982, dinner was $100 a person. That exposed me to a whole other world.

Those experiences helped to mold my relationship with money in a way that persists today. I gained an appreciation for how hard one must work to be successful and to save. When couples come to see me, I understand that it took them years of hard work to accumulate their retirement savings. I think back to my childhood and what I had to do to make just a couple of bucks.

Everybody has a story like that. Everyone's relationship with money is different, and it influences how they manage their resources. Most of us can think of a time long ago that began to shape our financial views. In our past are clues to what drives us, and when we understand that, we can see more clearly where we want to go—how we want our money to work for us.

HOPES, AMBITIONS, DREAMS

At some point in life (the earlier the better), people realize their working years won't go on forever, and perhaps soon, they will be retiring. So they start to save, unsure how much money they should be putting away weekly or monthly or what target they should be aiming to hit.

Many people just put away what they feel is their obligation to save. Some put away enough to maximize their employer's contribution to their 401(k) plan. Some don't think about it at all until retirement is staring them in the face. That is often when they come to me for their first visit. They typically are individuals or couples, several years from retirement, who realize they need guidance.

The majority of financial professionals will greet you and quickly get down to a point-blank question: "So how much money do you need to live on?" Husband and wife are likely to look at each other and shrug. A typical suggestion is that you should figure on a retirement income that is perhaps 70 percent of what you currently are making. The advisor may advocate a formula based on some study recommending a "safe" withdrawal rate of 3 or 4 percent of the prospective retiree's portfolio. Then, after Social Security and other income sources are figured in, if the result reaches the 70 percent threshold, all (supposedly) is well.

This is no way to plan a retirement. I believe it is a backward approach. It looks at the money first and then defines the lifestyle you can have. Notice that using this approach, what you want out of life seems like almost an afterthought. Your lifestyle is determined by a preset formula created in some faraway ivory tower. That's what you get with such a planning-by-numbers strategy. It is generic and pays little attention to your individual situation.

I think again of Paula, the woman in the chapter 1, who retired from her executive job and pursued her dreams. Before she came to me, her first advisor told her she didn't meet the 70-percent-of-current-income criterion and therefore should give up on this notion of retiring.

Since when? On what reality is that based? Here's another idea: Suppose we start out by talking about how you see your life unfolding in the next thirty years. What does retirement look like to you? What are your hopes and ambitions and dreams for you and your family? What is your vision of retirement?

In other words, we need to define your desired lifestyle first, and *then* we can figure out how to work the numbers to get there. Only when you know what you want to do can you determine how much it will cost.

We need to position your money to meet the realities of the life you anticipate. If you need 70 percent or more of your current income at the beginning of retirement, will that still be the case when you are seventy-five or eighty? Probably not. For some people, the 70 percent target will hold true. Others will need a lot less. Some might need considerably more, but only for the first few years—while they are indulging themselves in their long-postponed travels, for example, or pursuing an expensive hobby—after which they will back off on their spending. There is no formula. So much depends upon what you will be doing with your newfound time.

TO THE HEART OF THE MATTER

This is your life. You're not a number. All those robo-advisors and number crunchers have been turning financial planning into a commodity. They simply peddle asset allocation models. They might do it cheaply, with their economies of scale, but you get what you pay for. You are flesh and blood, and you deserve a plan tailored to your aspirations in life, not some sterile algorithm that will never be able to understand what truly matters to you.

These are the sort of questions—about values, goals, and relationships—that I would ask you at our very first meeting:

- **♀** What's important to you about money and why?
- **♀** What are your top accomplishments? What would you like them to be?
- **♀** What are your personal goals?
- **♀** What do you do (or want to do) for your children? For your parents? For other family members or close friends?
- **♀** Which family relationships (spouse, children, siblings, parents, etc.) are the most important to you?

These are questions that get to the heart of the matter. They serve as a springboard for people to engage in deep reflections on where they have been, where they expect to go, and why they feel it's important to get there. It comes down to getting your life priorities in order. What was the point in setting all that money aside? How do you intend to use it during your lifetime? Are you expecting to leave anything to your family, or to charity?

On the next page you will find my mind map. It is the script I use when I work with clients to discover their vision for retirement: what is important to them and who is important to them.

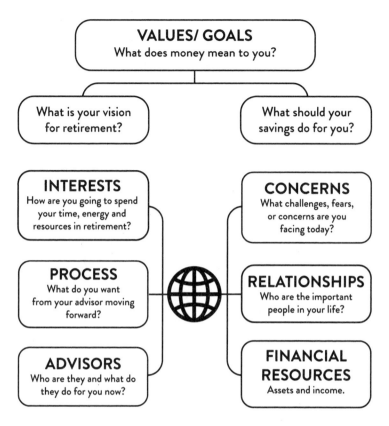

IN YOUR PERFECT WORLD

You have a multitude of choices. When you wake up in the morning, you can stay in bed all day, if you choose, or you can jump out of bed and head out to change the world. You can tackle that honey-do list, take an art or woodworking class, or shop for antiques at the flea market. Now, it's true you will need to stay within the bounds of what your income will allow you to do, but you should not be limiting yourself before you even consider the possibilities. I ask people to tell me about what they see as their perfect world in retirement.

I was talking with a couple, Linda and Jim, who were preparing for their retirement. Both were still working. Linda had just returned from an Alaskan cruise. She assumed that in a year or two, after she and Jim were both retired, they wouldn't be able to afford such trips anymore.

"Well, in your perfect world, do you see yourself still taking these types of trips?" I asked. Linda said she certainly did. "And how much would that cost a year?" She figured about $5,000.

"Since I'm hearing how important that is to you," I said, "why don't we just figure that expense into your retirement plan for now—even if it is every other year. Let's not just toss it aside as an impossibility."

Such is the case with many people. They have things they want to do, but they tend to rule them out at the start. Most advisors would applaud that attitude. It's easier (and more profitable) for them when the money stays in your portfolio. I believe that a better approach is to encourage a closer look before abandoning a dream.

I recently worked with a couple, Tom and Ellen, who had a seven-figure retirement fund. They were nervous about what might become of it. They knew it was a lot of money, but they were quite aware of how easily it could just disappear if they weren't careful. "We're going to put together a plan so that you will know what will be happening with your money and where it needs to be," I told them. That's what we call a Wealth Strategy.

Over the course of several weeks, we structured a comprehensive Wealth Strategy. We included some guaranteed income along with a variety of investments with appropriate levels of risk. I educated them about all the risks—not just investment risks. We looked at inflation, taxes, health care issues, estate concerns, and much more. Today they're off and running, enjoying the best years of their lives in retirement. They have been freed from their uncertainty. No longer are they afraid of going out to have a good time. That's what I try to do for people. I give them permission to spend their money, within reason. Isn't that what you deserve?

THE POWER OF CLARITY

Tom and Ellen could enjoy their retirement because they had clarity: Clarity of purpose. Clarity in how they would generate income. Clarity in the way they understood the many risks that wait for them down the road and the way they were armed with a strategy to protect their dream lifestyle. Once you gain clarity, you regain confidence, and the fun can begin. You can set out on that journey joyfully. Not only do you know your destination, but you know you can afford the gas.

As I pointed out, even highly affluent families still worry about their money, even if they have a billion dollars in the pot. They still recognize that they must handle it responsibly, and at that level of wealth, their focus generally tends to be on managing it efficiently so the fortune might last for generations. These folks have advanced beyond the accumulation stage and are firmly in the preservation and distribution stage, and in that sense, they share the mind-set of the typical retiree.

Once, when these families were emerging into wealth, they focused first on growing their money, second on getting income from it, and third on protecting it. Now, having risen so high and with so much to lose, they focus first on protecting their money and then on generating income and perhaps growing it. The family lifestyle has been secured, and the emphasis is on maintaining it.

Many people of retirement age will recognize that they too have shifted in their priorities, but the changing mind-set is more than financial in nature. Highly affluent families also become concerned with legacy issues. They want to make sure the money passes efficiently to future generations, and they want to be sure that those heirs will be worthy recipients who are well prepared for the responsibility. They begin to think more in terms of family values and how to do right by their children. Will the money help them or harm them?

These issues also preoccupy many retirees—not just the wealthiest. They are of an age when big-picture issues become more important. What's it all about? What was the purpose in working so hard all those years?

Unlike an asset allocation model or financial plan, a Wealth Strategy encompasses much more than money, although money is central to it all. It deals with investments, income generation, withdrawal strategies, tax management, health care issues, and legacy and estate concerns.

Too often, a financial plan begins and ends with an investment strategy. Sure, it may align your investments with your risk tolerance. It might also target a withdrawal percentage. But without first exploring why you saved all this money, can you truly be confident your future is secure? After all, what is the point of money if it can't advance your purposes?

In other words, your money is there to serve you. The only way we can make sure that it will do so is to define explicitly how you wish to be served.

FACING THE TRUTH

Many of us do not want to deal with our money and our future. Even as we approach retirement, we procrastinate. Perhaps we would rather have no news than to confront the possibility that we made poor decisions or that someone took advantage of us.

Such people may not want to hear, for example, that someone who they believed was a friend did them wrong. I met a couple who needed to draw $40,000 a year from their portfolio for their living expenses. They had variable annuities and other messy investments with hidden fees and other expenses totaling more than $50,000 a year. In other words, they were paying themselves less than they were paying their advisor.

You should never get upset about hearing the facts about your investments. I firmly believe you made the best decisions at the time with the information you were given, and you should believe this too. When families meet with me for the first time, I explain that I will be giving them new information about their situation and that it's time to reevaluate. It's time to set aside emotion—never mind the regrets. We must proceed rationally and decide whether you need to go in a different direction. This will empower you and allow you to feel in control of your financial situation. It is human to make mistakes. Smart people learn from their mistakes and take the opportunity to reevaluate their situation and change course when necessary.

I often wondered why most of us will readily get a second opinion for a medical procedure or how much it will cost to fix our car, but we avoid getting a second opinion about our finances like it was the Black Death. You deserve a second opinion. You have a right to know if everything is working as it should or if you need a course correction before it's too late.

Planning for a thriving retirement is too important a matter to put off. An ostrich might feel safe with its head in the ground, but it leaves its feathery rump exposed and vulnerable to predators. It's high time to take effective action, before it's too late.

Your financial security hinges on whether your vision for retirement is realistic, how well you have prepared for the risks you could face, and how you handle those risks along the way. Working with families in my practice, we have faced illness, sudden loss of a loved one, devastating acts of nature, and much more together. Those are a challenge for even the best of plans.

Don't let your dreams be dashed because of a misguided belief that such things only happen to someone else. When my mother was planning her trip of a lifetime to China, the last thing on her mind was that she might have advanced cancer. Troubles visit us all. Be prepared.

THE RISK OF NOT KNOWING

Throughout the rest of the book, we will look at a variety of risks that can threaten the financial security of your retirement. My goal—my mission—is to help you make your vision of the future of retirement a reality. I will help make sure you have carefully thought through the risks, the challenges, and the obstacles that stand in your way. You only go through retirement once.

The biggest risk of all is not knowing where you are going. I have found that many people lack this knowledge, and I'm here to help you find your way. I've met couples who imagine they can go places that their resources could never take them. They clearly are at risk not only of a big disappointment but also of a depleted portfolio. They have a vision too grand to support. Others severely limit their vision or do not even entertain one, because they're running scared. They suspect that they don't have enough money to see them through, even though they often have plenty and just don't know it. Their lifelong relationship with money has been to scrimp, and that mind-set continues into retirement. In their accumulation years, their frugality served to build sizable savings. But in their distribution years, unable to see a purpose and goal for that money, their frugality only limits their dreams.

I have helped both types of couples determine, realistically, where they are. I help them to see just what their money can do for them and caution them to use it wisely. Upon retirement, you often are sitting on a large sum of money and tend to feel generous. That is honorable, of course, but I've seen people become overly generous. Their children and others ask them for money for this or that, and it's $15,000 here and $5,000 there and "yes" to all requests. Without a disciplined plan for the use of their money, they are chipping away at their future and are at risk of destroying it.

Let's say you give away $30,000. Sure, the kids may have their reasons for needing it, but you have yours, too. That money will be gone forever. Not only do you give up the use of the money but also everything you could have earned on it in the future. This is called the opportunity cost of money. Most people never think about opportunity cost when giving away their money. They think only of how much they want to gift, spend, or lend. When you figure in the opportunity cost, that $30,000 is more like a $50,000 or $60,000 drain on your financial future.

I tell it like it is. I firmly believe that everyone has the right to spend their money any way they want, but my responsibility is to remind you that we charted a path for your future and to point out when you veer too far off your path. If you begin to spend twice as much as planned, your money will not last.

I understand that it can be hard to say no when loved ones ask for help. I tell people to put the blame on me. When the kids want money, tell them, "My financial advisor says I can't do that." That's the sort of discipline that will keep you on track. When you know where you are going, I know you will take the necessary steps to get there.

STEADY AS SHE GOES

A good Wealth Strategy is not meant to be left sitting on a shelf. Its proper function is to help you organize your life, and so it is essential to work with it actively and to keep it updated. Life changes. A plan must be regularly revisited and reevaluated. It has been said that the battle plan changes as soon as the first bullet is fired. Or, as boxer Mike Tyson purportedly put it, "Everyone has a plan until they get hit." That's all the more reason to be prepared. You need to be able to make good decisions and adjust your approach.

Think of it this way: A flight from Los Angeles to New York is not a straight line—far from it. The pilot needs to make regular adjustments. Wind direction and air traffic patterns will have much to do with how the pilot goes about staying on course. The natural curvature and spinning of the earth must be factored into the equation. Without those adjustments, the plane could end up not in New York but perhaps in Nova Scotia, or parts unknown.

Like the pilot, I make many adjustments to help keep families on the right path. We take a close look and assemble a detailed plan that identifies where they need to be along the way. How much income will they require? How much money must be in their accounts? What is the best procedure for withdrawing it?

You do not want to wait fifteen years and then find you are half a million dollars short of where you needed to be. Adjustments along the way are essential. In fact, my contracts with clients include a paragraph requiring them to tell me about anything significant that changes in their lives so that I will be able to keep them on track.

You cannot know whether your strategy is working unless you pay attention to it. If you expect to be at a certain point in two years, or five years, or ten years, you will not know whether you have succeeded until you get to those milestones and look around. Preparing for retirement and creating a Wealth Strategy are meaningless without carefully monitoring and measuring your progress. A plan is pointless unless you use it as a means to help you get to your destination.

To plan for the retirement of your dreams, you need to keep the end in mind and work backward from there to fill in the details and choose the appropriate strategies, based upon your resources and opportunities, to make it all happen.

QUESTIONS TO CONSIDER

- What early experiences shaped the way you think about money?

- Do you think you will need less money in retirement, or more? Why?

- How would you define a successful retirement?

- Can you identify a purpose for your money?

- Who are the people and what are the causes you care about most? How do you wish to support them?

- When would you like to know whether you are on track to meet your life goals?

Chapter 4

IT'S A DIFFERENT GAME (LONGEVITY)

How long does your money need to last?

As we live longer, the traditional model of retirement planning has changed dramatically. Social Security's future is questionable, particularly for younger people. Pensions today are rare. That leaves it up to you to fill the gap with your own investments, whether you're up to the challenge are not. For most people, the ubiquitous 401(k)-type plan has become the primary means for retirement savings.

J oe and Becky, both sixty-nine, had come in for the semi-annual review of their Wealth Strategy. We were discussing the best way to manage the distributions that they soon would be required to withdraw from their 401(k) account, after reaching age seventy. As we were chatting, Becky offered this observation: "I never thought this is what it'd be like to be almost seventy. I feel much younger than I expected at this age."

Many people are pleasantly surprised to find, well into retirement, that their energy hasn't faded. They remember their own grandparents at age seventy and assumed life would be slowing down along with their bodies. Typically, it's still full speed ahead. People are living longer, and the Internet and social media have made the world seem to be both a smaller and a bigger place. We can keep in touch with distant friends far more easily, and technology has expanded opportunities for keeping busy. "I don't know how I ever had time to hold down a job," folks often tell me.

If you're 65 today, the probability of living to a specific age or beyond

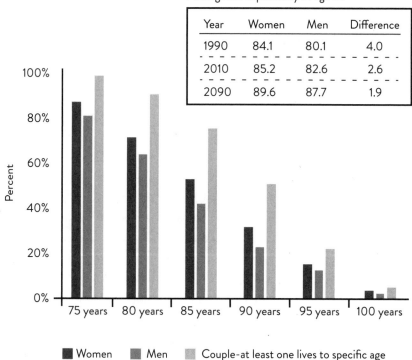

Average life expectancy at age 65

Year	Women	Men	Difference
1990	84.1	80.1	4.0
2010	85.2	82.6	2.6
2090	89.6	87.7	1.9

Women ■ Men ■ Couple–at least one lives to specific age ▨

That's the good news. We can enjoy extended and generally healthier, active lives thanks to modern medicine. We can look forward to a retirement that our parents and grandparents might never have imagined. However, every silver lining comes with a cloud. Yes, the good news is that we are living longer. And now for the bad news: We are living longer. We have to pay for all those years.

Centenarians, once rare, are becoming far more common. Retirement no longer means saying that final farewell a few years after the working days end. People are living decades into their post-employment days. They're busy living, and they're busy spending.

Longevity has dramatically changed the fundamental nature of retirement planning. The underlying reason isn't complicated: When you live longer, your money must last longer. That dramatically changes the challenges you will face in retirement. Unfortunately, many people still hold fast to a retirement model that was based on a much shorter lifespan. They fail to adequately consider the potential of three decades or more of retirement, much of which is likely to be very active.

Longevity has a ripple effect. It's called *inflation*. Inflation would not be such a concern if its erosive effect on retirement savings persisted for only a few years. However, a 3 percent inflation rate (which is about average) over a twenty-four-year retirement can cut purchasing power in half. In other words, if you retired at sixty, by eighty-four you would need twice the dollars to maintain the same standard of living. Over time, inflation can destroy wealth. Longevity also amplifies other issues, like the toll taxation will take on your investments. Medical insurance and end-of-life care issues take on greater significance, because an aging body requires more maintenance, and that comes at a cost.

As you can see, our greater longevity affects a wide range of retirement decisions. How, then, could anyone expect that the strategies of two or three decades ago would work well today? The old methods need to yield to a new way of thinking. Today's retirees need an approach that is up to the challenge of making their money last. It's a new game.

IT'S UP TO YOU NOW

In previous generations, the typical retirement planning approach was the so-called "three-legged stool." It was a relatively stable structure: one leg of the stool was the employer pension, or defined-benefit plan; another leg was the Social Security benefit; and the third leg was the personal savings and investments accumulated over the years. You could rest comfortably on that stool, reasonably confident that you would have a regular income flow for as long as you lived.

Many people who are currently retired still do have pensions, but those are becoming a thing of the past. Most who are planning now for their retirement don't have a pension. They still have the Social Security leg of the stool, but they wonder whether they can depend on it to prop them up in the years ahead. They have lost faith in the system and don't want to count on a benefit they suspect might one day vanish.

With one leg of the stool falling off and another leg splintering, you are left with only your personal savings to produce lifelong income. Your former employer probably won't be looking out for you. The government is likely to continue to tighten the Social Security rules as the system struggles. In other words, you should depend on yourself to secure a stable retirement. The responsibility is on your shoulders. Let's take a closer look at how longevity affects the three-legged stool.

SOCIAL SECURITY

Our longevity is at the root of the problem with the Social Security system. The program was a centerpiece of Roosevelt's New Deal initiatives of the 1930s, when people typically didn't live all that long after their working days were through. There were many young workers in those days who could be taxed to support the relatively few retirees who were receiving benefits.

Over the decades, the ratio of workers to retirees has become far lower than originally projected. In 1950, about sixteen workers supported each retiree. Now, only about three workers are paying into the system for each beneficiary, and as baby boomers begin to retire in droves, that ratio inevitably will get tighter.

The demographic shift is bound to lead to further political efforts to shore up the system. The Social Security trust fund currently is projected to be depleted by 2034 unless taxes are increased, benefits are cut, or other measures are taken. This is clearly a system in trouble.

Nonetheless, I believe that anyone who is age fifty or over can plan on receiving a Social Security benefit that is reasonably close to what has been promised. The big question for today's retiree is not if the Social Security system will last but how you will deal with the impact of inflation on your Social Security benefit.

Because the Social Security system is in trouble, the government is finding a lot of creative ways to bolster the system. Some suggestions include further raising the full retirement age, which already has been raised to sixty-seven for people born in 1960 or later. The government could impose income tax on an increasing percentage of benefits. Originally, those benefits were nontaxable, but today up to 85 percent could be subject to tax. In other words, we're taxed twice: when the money goes into the system and again when it comes out.

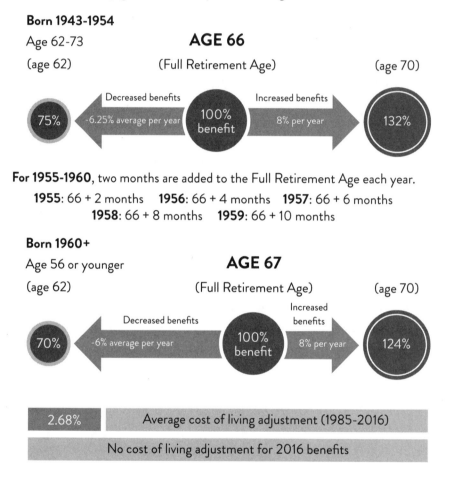

Born 1943-1954

Age 62-73   **AGE 66**

(age 62)   (Full Retirement Age)   (age 70)

Decreased benefits   Increased benefits

75%   -6.25% average per year   100% benefit   8% per year   132%

For 1955-1960, two months are added to the Full Retirement Age each year.
1955: 66 + 2 months   **1956**: 66 + 4 months   **1957**: 66 + 6 months
1958: 66 + 8 months   **1959**: 66 + 10 months

Born 1960+

Age 56 or younger   **AGE 67**

(age 62)   (Full Retirement Age)   (age 70)

Decreased benefits   Increased benefits

70%   -6% average per year   100% benefit   8% per year   124%

2.68%   Average cost of living adjustment (1985-2016)

No cost of living adjustment for 2016 benefits

For the time being, the government's focus hasn't been on reducing benefits but rather on limiting the increase in benefits. This is what concerns me the most. What this means is that there likely will be more years in which retirees get a zero or close-to-zero increase in their cost-of-living adjustment, as was the case in 2010, 2011, and 2016. We can also expect further measures like the recent restrictions placed on spousal benefits.

The combination of longevity and smaller increases in Social Security over time means that your Social Security benefit will represent a small and smaller part of your income as you get older. According to the Social Security Administration, the average wage earner can expect his or her benefit to replace 40 percent of preretirement earnings. However, I do not believe you should base your planning on that expectation, especially for your later retirement years. In general, Social Security is bound to play an increasingly diminished role in retirement planning.

Unfortunately, most financial planning software does not take this into consideration. This creates what I call a *false positive*. The current planning software is still using old assumptions. This means most financial plans still rely on Social Security as a major income source for much longer than we can comfortably assume. If you are not careful, a plan showing that your income and assets will last into your nineties may run out of money years earlier than expected. This is the result of incorrectly adjusting for the changes in Social Security benefits over time.

FLIPPING THE RETIREMENT SWITCH

One of your first decisions when contemplating retirement will be when to flip the switch to begin receiving your Social Security benefit. The earliest you can apply is at age sixty-two, but that comes at a price. You could be penalized up to 25 percent of the benefit you would have earned.[3] To get your entire earned benefit, you need to wait until full retirement age (typically between sixty-six and sixty-seven, based on your birth year). You also could choose to wait as late

---

3 "Retirement Planner: Can You Take Your Benefits Before Full Retirement Age?" Social Security Administration, https://www.ssa.gov/planners/retire/applying2.html.

as age seventy. Your benefit increases by 8 percent every year past full retirement age.

You can find many online calculators that claim to help you determine the best time to begin your Social Security benefit. You punch in your basic information, including how much money you expect to need for your living expenses, and the calculators will spit out figures and dates for your consideration. For example, you can find out how much you would receive in total benefits by age ninety if you pursue one strategy versus another. The Social Security Administration's own website (www.ssa.gov) includes a variety of calculators to help people determine the right timing and the approximate amount of benefits they might expect.

Use those calculators with great caution. Keep in mind that effective money management is much more than a simple math equation. The question to ask yourself at all times when comparing strategies is, "Which one will have a greater impact on my life?" Here's an easy guideline: If you need the money to survive, then take your benefit now. If you have other resources that are sufficient to support you, you can consider postponing the benefit.

However, you can't make this decision in a vacuum. Look carefully at how your Social Security benefit would affect all your other retirement income sources. Will it complement your overall income, or jeopardize it? If you accept your benefit now, will it push you into a higher tax bracket? Before taking the benefit, perhaps you first should first consider drawing down on your 401(k) or other qualified account, keeping in mind that after age seventy, you will be required to begin withdrawing that money and paying those long-deferred taxes. A good strategy not only gets the most money out of the Social Security system but also keeps your tax bill as low as possible.

In other words, before deciding when to take your Social Security benefit, you need to determine what that would mean for the rest of your plan. That's what a Wealth Strategy is all about! Many people make the mistake of looking only at how much they can get from Social Security without assessing the impact on the other elements of their financial planning. They try to calculate how they can get the most total dollars out of the system but fail to consider the tax consequences and the best overall strategy. By jumping for the money, they risk losing a big chunk of it.

The question should not be, "How can I work the system to get the most from Social Security?" Rather, it should be, "How can I get the most out of all of my financial resources?" Most of the aforementioned calculators address the first question, but they can't tell you the answer to the second one. The best, most comprehensive approach depends on a variety of factors and requires a full review by someone who understands the specifics of your family situation. It requires information about your situation that is much more sophisticated than what you can enter on a computer screen.

There is no standard answer to the second question, which is one of the reasons I developed the Wealth Strategy concept. The formulas fail when it comes to finesse. If you go to a Social Security seminar and someone offers to whip up an easy report based on how much money you want and the age when you'd like to retire, you may not be dealing with someone who is looking out for your best interest. That person is leading you toward a decision without conducting a full analysis of your financial situation. Does he or she know how much money you have in tax-deferred, taxable, and tax-free accounts? How about rental income? Pensions? A pension, if not managed properly, can push you into a higher tax bracket. What will be the extent and timing of your 401(k) distributions, and how will that influence your Social Security decision? How should you be factoring inflation into your retirement plan? What about when you lose some of your benefit due to the death of a spouse? How is that factored in?

Howard and Jeanette, a couple who recently came to see me, found out too late that they made a mistake. They have a retirement lifestyle that calls for about $100,000 a year. Howard, who is now sixty-eight, switched on his Social Security benefit early, because it helped them reach that income level without touching the money in his 401(k) plan. As we reviewed their overall finances, it was clear what would happen in a few years (at age seventy-and-a-half), when he would be forced to begin the required minimum distributions from that 401(k). Although they only needed $100,000 a year, their tax return would be showing $200,000 in income because of the forced distributions from his 401(k) plan and other factors. Howard's earlier decision on when to take his Social Security benefit would contribute to pushing him into a higher tax bracket when he reaches age seventy and a half. Had he structured his planning differently, gradually withdrawing some of that tax-deferred money, he might have saved significantly on taxes.

Again, this is not something that the typical Social Security calculator will reveal. The elements of your financial life are interconnected and interdependent, like an ecosystem, and the Social Security benefit is just one of the variables in a healthy balance. It must be considered in conjunction with the nature of your other investments and their risk level, your tax situation, your income needs, and your goals. Some of the key considerations are these: How long do you expect to live? How long do people in your family tend to live? What is the current state of your health?

A PENSIONER'S DILEMMA

While many of us do not have corporate pensions, there are still a significant number of us who can expect to receive a pension at retirement. Let me tell you the fictional tale of Mary Jane, a teacher who learned that having both a pension and a 403(b) retirement plan would have some unanticipated consequences.

As a teacher with tenure, Mary Jane will receive a pension and Social Security benefit at retirement. One day, a friend asked her whether she should contribute to her 403(b) plan to save for retirement, deferring the taxes. "Of course you should," Mary Jane said without missing a beat. "Everyone knows that you should put as much as possible into your 403(b) plan."

Sarah, another teacher, overheard the conversation and tapped Mary Jane on the shoulder. "Here's something to think about," she told her colleague. "Let me ask you a question: Why are you putting money away in your 403(b)?"

"To save money on taxes, of course."

"But aren't you just postponing your taxes to be calculated at a later date?" Sarah asked.

"Well yes, now that I think about it," Mary Jane replied. "What I'm trying to do is arrange it so I'll be paying taxes in the future, when I'm in a lower tax bracket."

And there lies the rub. Will she be in a lower tax bracket? I have worked with many teachers, federal and state workers, and police. When they add their pension and Social Security benefits together, many find that they are in the same or a higher tax bracket. And when they reach age seventy and a half, they are also forced to take money out of their 403(b) because of required minimum distributions. Instead of being in a lower tax bracket now that they are retired, they find that they are paying more in taxes than before retirement, even though they do not need the cash! Instead of saving them money, that tax-deferred retirement plan actually cost them thousands of dollars.

The next logical question for people in Mary Jane's situation would be this: "So if I don't put my money into a 403(b) plan, what should I do?" I recommend a tax-free account that is principal-protected and can grow at a reasonable rate. That creates a tax-free income at retirement, as long as the rules are carefully followed.

Remember, just because everyone is doing it doesn't make it right. Tax-deferred accounts can be great for some and not so good for others. Folks with pensions are in a unique position, and the conventional wisdom of saving as much as you can in your retirement plan may not work well for them.

PENSION OPTIONS—NOT AN EASY CHOICE

There are an awful lot of decisions that need to be made when you retire with a pension. Most pensions give you the option of taking a lump sum benefit. This means you can just receive a large, one-time distribution from the pension fund instead of lifetime monthly payments.

If you opt for taking a monthly payment, you are faced with another set of decisions. Do you take the pension benefit for a single life? This means when you die, the pension ends. Do you choose an option that includes a continuation benefit? This means that when you die, your spouse will receive some or all of the pension benefit you were receiving before your death.

The correct option is different for everyone. While most pension plans have representatives who will counsel you on your options, they may not (and have no obligation to) act in your best interest. In fact, they may be pushing a pension benefit option that is better for the plan than for you.

This is where working with an independent financial advisor is very important. This is one of the areas I spend a lot of time dealing with, because so many families I work with face this issue. Later in the book, I will discuss how to choose an advisor who best suits your needs.

THE RISE OF THE 401(K)

The demise of pensions in our society is often associated with the rise of the 401(k) and similar employer-sponsored retirement plans that have proliferated in recent decades. For many families, the 401(k) has replaced the pension as the bedrock of retirement planning. Few companies continue to offer pensions to their existing employees—today, pensions exist mostly in the public sector. Instead of the employer investing in a retirement fund on the workers' behalf, workers are now investing on their own behalf from a menu of mutual funds presented to them by their employer, who often provides a matching contribution.

The genesis of the 401(k) movement was an obscure provision that Congress added to the tax code in 1978, taking effect a few years later. This new part of the code—section 401(k)—was intended to offer taxpayers a break on income that they elected to receive as deferred compensation. Within a few years, benefits consultant Ted Benna recognized the opportunity to use the provision to create a retirement savings vehicle for his own employees.

The Johnson Companies, Benna's employer, implemented a very basic 401(k) plan that did not look much like the plans of today. It was a basic plan, without the many investment choices that many plans offer today. Little did he know then that his initiative would become the basis of our country's retirement system. I met Benna in 1991, when I was working with the Rosenwald family. Now, twenty-plus years later, I find myself with an office on the same block as Benna's company in Newtown, Pennsylvania.

By the early 1990s, nearly half of large American firms were offering their employees a 401(k)-type plan or were considering one.[4] Soon, companies large and small were taking advantage of this opportunity for both themselves and their employees. The old, defined-benefit pension system was on the way out. The defined-contribution system was becoming the preferred program for employees to save for retirement.

During the great bull market of the 1990s, many companies saw huge run-ups in their pension account values, and some felt that they no longer needed to fund them. It seemed that the rising market would go on forever. Then along came the bursting of the dot-com bubble in 2001–2002 and the severe recession later in the decade. Realizing the difficulty in meeting their continuing pension obligations, more and more companies joined the 401(k) bandwagon, shifting the obligation for retirement account funding more toward the employee. It was an opportunity to rid themselves of the responsibility of taking care of their employees as well as the liability of funding a pension plan. Employers shut their pensions down and froze the values, telling their employees that they would have to save on their own, with a bit of matching help from the company.

In effect, employees with a 401(k) plan are expected to manage their money in the same way large companies once managed their

---

4 "History of 401(k) Plans: An Update," Employee Benefit Research Institute (February 2005). https://www.ebri.org/pdf/publications/facts/0205fact.a.pdf.

pension funds. Employees lack the resources to hire advisors and consultants to help them choose the right investment strategies for their needs and retirement goals. They're on their own.

It is unfortunate that a great many people simply don't know what they're doing on their own. They've been given this role and a menu of investment options—now what? While being interviewed on the Fox Business channel, I raised the issue of the severe lack of investment education in our schools. With the responsibility of saving for retirement being shifted from the employer to the employee, you would think it would be a much greater priority.

We are approaching the fourth decade of the 401(k) era, and many of those young employees who saw the 401(k) plan introduced years ago are now getting ready to make their first withdrawals. They soon will see whether there was wisdom in their investment ways and whether they made the right choices to grow a nest egg sufficient for retirement. The time has also come to pay the tax piper. We will take a closer look at those deferred-tax ramifications later on in the book.

Although these retirement plans brought in a tidal wave of new investors, they were not necessarily smart investors. Many who chose to enroll failed to sufficiently diversify, often keeping most of their money in company stock. They sometimes tucked their money away into funds with exorbitant fees, not recognizing how much of their money was being drained away.

Some employees simply don't participate in their company plan, and for those who do, the savings rate is often woefully low, with account balances not nearly large enough to support a comfortable retirement in the way that pensions did for previous generations.

I am often asked, "How much should I contribute to my company plan?" My advice is this: It depends. Yes, you should participate in your company's retirement savings plan, especially if they provide a matching contribution. But that might not be enough. Make sure you work with a qualified financial professional to determine not just how much you should be putting away for retirement but also where it should be invested. A good rule of thumb is 15 to 20 percent of your gross salary.

Sometimes it makes the most sense to put additional dollars into your 401(k), but sometimes your additional savings should be put in other types of accounts, called *nonqualified* or *tax-free* accounts. Always remember: All the money you put in your retirement account, including all that you earn over the years, will be taxed one day when it is distributed to you, your spouse, or your heirs. Uncle Sam will want his cut.

The 401(k) has become the primary vehicle by which Americans save for retirement. You are able to contribute regularly and build a substantial account over the years, tax issues notwithstanding. Without it, many people would be saving little or nothing, and for that reason alone it is a valuable addition to the retirement planning toolbox. But it's not the solution. It's part of the solution. To ensure sufficient resources for a long and enjoyable retirement, you need to take responsibility today so your money serves you well down the line. You need a plan. You need a Wealth Strategy.

NO EASY SOLUTIONS

I could fill pages about interest rates, stock market volatility, the demise of pensions, the rise of 401(k)s, and many other factors, but none of those caused the significant change in how we should all approach planning for retirement in the twenty-first century. Longevity, the mere fact that we are living longer, has made so many other issues that impact our money so important. It is because money must last for many more years that interest rates, taxes, and market volatility have become more of a worry.

Though the explanation for why planning for retirement has become much more challenging, there are no easy answers on how to deal with the details of generating income for a lifetime, managing taxes, dealing with inflation, protecting against market volatility, paying for the high cost of health care, and making sure our money gets to the people we choose and not the government. I understand why people might be tempted to reach for easy solutions. They want to make a decision and be done with it so they can move on and enjoy life. It is much more likely, however, that they will enjoy life if they plan correctly. That is why they need an advisor who is firmly on their side, is looking out for their best interest, and is knowledgeable about all the issues you will face as a retiree in the twenty-first century. You need someone more qualified to help you than a product salesperson or the clerk down at the Social Security office.

Certainly, your advisor should be made of flesh and blood, not bits and bytes. The trend toward robo-advisors reflects our society's prevailing desire for simple solutions. Artificial intelligence has not reached the point where a computer can look you in the eye with compassion, understanding, and discernment. The tools of technology are highly valuable, but they must remain within the context of a human relationship.

Investing for your retirement is a daunting responsibility. Many people lack the skills and desire to meet that challenge, and that's quite all right, as we each have our own area of wisdom and expertise. Like a smart CEO, the wise investor will delegate the job to a qualified advisor. Despite the loss of pensions and the insecurity of Social Security, those who proceed with wisdom and good counsel should do well.

So much has changed. Even the language of retirement planning shows the new mind-set in the age of the 401(k). Many people today think first about how big a pile of money they have rather than how much income they will have. In the pension days, people talked about how much cash they would be getting regularly to support what they wanted to do in retirement. Today, they talk about the size of their account. The challenge is to refocus on income. It is not necessarily how much money you amass that matters so much as how much income you can generate as you pursue your retirement dreams. In the next chapter, we will talk about keeping the cash flowing.

QUESTIONS TO CONSIDER

- How do you believe inflation will affect your retirement?
- What is your biggest financial concern?
- Have you investigated the best time to apply for your Social Security?
- What are the factors involved in determining when to begin your Social Security benefits?
- What are some of the ripple effects of longevity that influence retirement planning?
- Do you feel that the financial advice you are receiving can and will help you realize your vision for retirement?
- If you have a pension, have you investigated and evaluated all your options?
- Have you investigated and evaluated what would happen to your Social Security and/or pension if you or your spouse dies?

Chapter 5

YOUR WEALTH STRATEGY

Where will my income come from?

It's not how much money you amass during your working years that matters most—it's how much cash flow you can produce for retirement. The income you need will depend on a variety of factors including longevity, inflation, taxes, market volatility, your health, and how much you hope to leave to your heirs.

"See all those ripples on the river?" the pilot asked me on a tour of the Alaskan wilds. I peered from the cockpit at the shimmering ribbon below us. "You might think it's the wind," he said, "but it's millions of fish. This is the salmon run." He explained their vital importance to the balance of nature. "The grizzlies, the eagles, the orca whales—they couldn't survive without the salmon," he said. "It all works together."

That's the central theme for effective retirement planning, as well. It, too, is a sort of ecosystem where various elements rely on one another. You must not ignore any of the risks to your financial future. Over the years of working with families I have determined that there are five key risks or concerns that could cost you a great deal if not accounted for in your retirement plan. Addressing these concerns is the basis for how and why I created the Wealth Strategy Approach.

THE RIGHT APPROACH

My undergraduate degree was in computer engineering, which taught me to be process-oriented. Skipping steps gets you in trouble. In the binary world, it all breaks down to ones and zeroes in infinitely complicated combinations. If you neglect the programming fundamentals, the computer is less than useless: garbage in, garbage out.

In engineering school, I was taught to do everything twice. You build a system and then go back to reexamine every stage, looking for anything that might go wrong in the process and spoil the outcome. There were many nights that I did not want to go over my work. I often thought it was good enough—until my classmates or my professor tested it. That's when I learned the hard lesson of always going over every solution twice. As my longtime friend John, a master carpenter, would say, "Measure twice, cut once."

Today I help families prepare for their future by creating a Wealth Strategy that considers the five key risks a retiree must address to be successful in retirement. Unlike your plain vanilla financial plan, a Wealth Strategy helps keep it all working together to produce enough wealth and income to meet their vision of retirement. Most people can't imagine what their lives will be like in retirement, let alone know just how much money they will need. Your idea of a successful retirement is likely different than your neighbor's, and therefore your investments will need to be different. You will have different priorities and differing perspectives on how to deal with risks. All those concerns together will determine the cash flow that is right for you.

YOUR INCOME IS THE REAL ISSUE

For years, you worked to build as big a nest egg as possible. You followed the prevailing wisdom. Now you need to use that money to support yourself. The grand total of what you have accumulated in your accounts matters less than how much you can get out of those accounts and into your pocket consistently for the rest of your life. No longer are you just trying to save and grow your money. It's time to draw an income from it.

Typically, people imagine that when they retire they can withdraw some percentage of their savings each year and still be set for life. A few even think that's 10 percent, because they believe they can invest as if we were still in the 1990s. That's a big gamble that they likely will lose. You often will hear that the "safe" or "sustainable" withdrawal rate is 4 percent—sometimes higher and sometimes lower. The researchers keep changing the rule of thumb, and the trend is downward. But even using a withdrawal rate of 3 or 4 percent, the results can surprise you.

Let's say that Jim Smith is planning on retiring at the end of the year. He and his wife decide a 4 percent withdrawal rate makes the most sense for their situation. They have $1 million dollars in their 401(k)s. If they take $40,000 a year to live on, they feel that they will have no trouble maintaining their current lifestyle.

After many years of hard work, the day Jim Smith retires finally arrives. He calls the 401(k) administrator and requests the $40,000 they will need to live on for their first year of retirement. For this example, we are going to assume that the Smith's top tax bracket is 20 percent.

A few days later, a deposit of $32,000 shows up in their checking account—$8,000 less than expected. Not a good thing at all. Why did this happen? Taxes!

When you withdraw money from a qualified account like an IRA or 401(k), you have to pay taxes on the money before you receive it. The Smiths had to withhold $8,000 to cover the tax bill. In order for the Smiths to receive $40,000 net from their 401(k), they may need to withdraw $50,000, which is actually a 5 percent withdrawal rate. Notice that the taxes on a $40,000 withdraw was $8,000, but on a $50,000 withdraw, it was $10,000. That's a 25 percent increase in taxes.

However, if the Smiths had their money in a tax-free account or used after-tax money, then when they request a $40,000 distribution they could end up with the whole $40,000 in their pocket. Here is something to think about. How will that extra $10,000 per year affect the Smith's retirement plan?

MORE THAN A MAGIC NUMBER

Here is another example of how only looking at how much you have in your accounts can be misleading.

I recently met with a couple in their early fifties who asked me to help them get their savings to $1.4 million. They figured that's what they needed to retire. "So what does that $1.4 million look like?" I asked. They looked puzzled.

"Well, maybe you're talking about $1.4 million in municipal bonds paying 5 percent, tax-free," I explained. "Or you might be putting it all in a 401(k) plan, or half of it in a Roth account. Or do you just have a regular taxable account at a brokerage? Have you considered how much of your money you want in the market, and whether any of it should be set aside for guaranteed income?"

I wanted them to see that there's much more to it than just reaching some magic number. "And when you start taking that money out," I continued, "we need to look at which of your accounts you will use first. If you're getting Social Security and a pension, how will we keep the taxes down? Will there be a capital gains issue if you start cashing in on that $1.4 million?"

Those are the sorts of questions you're not likely to hear from the folks at the big financial institutions or an annuity-only insurance broker. They want to sell you something, whether it's an annuity or an index fund or whatever they are featuring this month. It's easier to treat everyone the same, as if everything were equal. They don't want to pull the curtain back and show you how it all works. That would just complicate things for them.

What you need to understand is that the real issue is implementing the best possible strategy to generate cash flow to meet your retirement needs. Back in the pension days, the focus for retirement planning was on cash flow and income. With the rise of 401(k) plans, the conversation switched to how much you have saved, or need to save, to retire comfortably. Retirement planning became a quest to achieve a number.

We need to get back to the cash flow conversation. The real concern is how much income your savings can produce for the rest of your life, and because no one knows how long that will be, you need to be willing to adjust along the way. During your working years, did you tell the boss how much to pay you, or did the boss tell you how much you would be paid? In other words, once you knew your income, your family adjusted your lifestyle to fit it.

You need not live in uncertainty. I've seen couples with plenty of money in the bank who count pennies, fearful they will live too long and run out of money. Others seem oblivious until they discover that they're out of money at age eighty. The solution in both cases is a Wealth Strategy that produces reliable income while considering how everything works together. You also need to update your plan every year, because, to put it simply, life happens.

You can find many advisors who will talk to you about investment performance from year to year, but few will show you how that translates into what you most need to know: how much income you will have available to live on. That's the real issue. I work out the details and tell you what you can reasonably spend every month. You can feel confident about using that money, knowing that we regularly review your overall situation to make sure you're still on track.

That's the sort of confidence that people felt with pensions. When you know that check will be coming in every month, you feel secure. When you're just looking at a pile of money, you feel the weight of all those questions and uncertain of what the future will bring.

CASH FLOW AND YOUR WEALTH STRATEGY

Your Wealth Strategy helps make sure you have enough income to live on to make your vision of retirement a reality. Earlier in the book, we talked about your vision for retirement, your purpose, and your goals outside of how much money you have accumulated. Now it is time to take a look at the numbers.

YOUR WEALTH STRATEGY

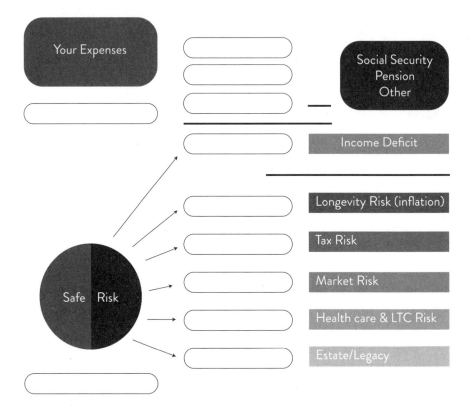

The chart above is a picture of what your Wealth Strategy needs to include.

To begin we need to inventory your savings—not just how much money you have but where it is. Is most of your money in a tax-deferred account like a 401(k) or IRA? Do you have taxable investments that have large capital gains or losses? Will your savings be available when you need it or will you incur a penalty or surrender charge to get your hands on it? These questions and much more are so important to understanding how and when you will access your saving during retirement.

Because it's not as simple as saying, "We've made it to $1 million, so we're good to go." The economy will change, your life will change, and the world will change. In the retirement ecosystem, all things work together. That's what people contemplating retirement must recognize. Some of the risk factors will matter more to different people, but you must take all of them into account, because they are interdependent. You just can't address just one risk factor at a time.

Now it's time to figure out how much income you need to support the lifestyle you want in retirement. Figuring out how much you need for living expenses doesn't need to be a complex exercise. You don't have to go through your old bills and statements. You just need your recent pay stubs. How much was your take-home check? How much goes into your checking or savings account for one month? Next, subtract any other savings you make, beyond what you put into your 401(k) plan. Then look at all your debt. Mortgage? Car payments? Credit cards? Will those still be around when you retire? If so, subtract your monthly debt payments from your cash flow number. The result is a number you can work with. In an ideal world, that is how much you need to live on in retirement.

But that's just the start. You also will need to consider what I call "add-backs," or the costs you face from **five key risk factors** you will face during your retirement:

1. inflation, which obviously becomes a bigger factor the longer you live;

2. taxes;

3. market volatility;

4. health care and long-term care; and

5. estate/legacy costs, or how much you intend to leave to your heirs.

All those will influence how long your money lasts. The question then becomes, which of these five risk factors are most significant to you? That is how you start to develop a Wealth Strategy. Your big risk factor might be taxes, particularly if virtually all your savings are in tax-deferred accounts. A big risk factor for everyone is inflation. Some are more concerned about market risk and volatility. Everyone's focus will be different.

You can calculate a number for each of your risk factors. For example, you can calculate the cost of inflation, and you can calculate taxes owed on tax-deferred accounts based on the required minimum distribution schedule. By doing so, you quantify each risk factor and get a more accurate picture of how much income you will need.

We start by determining how much income your investments must generate. You start by totaling your expenses and subtracting known revenue streams (usually Social Security or a pension). The result is your income deficit: the amount that your investments need to produce.

From there we can calculate your "minimum retirement rate of return." That's an important number to know. Let's say, for example, that your deficit is $10,000 a month, or $120,000 a year. If your investment pool is $1 million, you need a 12 percent return, which is obviously a lot to expect of any portfolio. A big number indicates that you should have some concerns about how long your money will last. A small number tells you you're doing pretty well.

It doesn't end there, however. It's not just a matter of how *much* you can generate from your investments for income. It's also a matter of *how* it is generated. When we talk about rate of return (what you make on your money), it is important to understand how it is achieved.

Rate of return usually has two components: yield, and the net of gains and losses from your investments. The yield is the cash produced by distributions, interest, and dividends. The return equals the yield plus gains or minus losses. Let's say you have an investment with a return of 5 percent and a yield of 1 percent. That means it must have 4 percent growth, year in and year out. Compare that with another investment that also has a 5 percent return but has a 3 percent yield, meaning the growth level needs to be only 2 percent. In retirement, the latter investment provides more security, because it generates more income and relies less on growth.

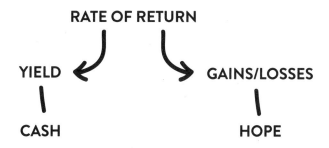

THE RIGHT MIX FOR YOU

Just as there are five risk factors you need to focus on when preparing for retirement, there are many different types of investments you can use. Some may be very tax efficient but not very liquid. Some may be very safe but produce a low return. Some investments may give you the potential to make a lot of money but can also lose a lot of money very quickly.

Imagine seeing this sign as you enter a store: *Low prices, great quality, super service—pick any two!* When you think about it, that's the way of the merchandising world. If you want good quality at a low price, don't expect the best of service. If you want both good quality and good service, you can expect to pay a premium. And if you are looking for efficient service and low prices, you can expect a fast-food kind of quality.

Likewise, every investment has some combination of three basic characteristics: its level of liquidity, or how quickly you can get your money; its level of safety from loss; and its potential for growth. Typically, you can get two of those, but not all three. A safe, liquid investment (such as a bank account) is unlikely to grow much. A liquid investment that offers growth (such as stock market securities) won't be protected from losses. If you want both safety and some growth, your investment will likely be less liquid (such as a long-term CD or fixed annuity).

Your retirement portfolio should have money in each of those categories. You should have some emergency cash. You should have some relatively safe investments that still give you lots of income. And you should have some money at risk so you have the potential for more gain. What's the proper mix for you? It depends on who you are, where you are at financially, and your comfort level.

I have found that most people are lacking in one area or another. They might have all their money in cash, or all in the market, or all in annuities. What they don't have is flexibility. They can't easily move between those investment worlds. Lacking a proper asset allocation, they can't react effectively to changes, either in the economy or in their personal situation.

A few years ago a good friend and advisor met with a couple for a second opinion meeting. The couple brought a grocery bag with piles of paper. After Tom had sorted through everything, he found contracts for 36 different annuities their current broker had sold them.

While both Tom and I use annuities in our practice, 36 annuities holding almost all the couples money did not seem like their broker was acting in their interest. Under this picture in Tom's officer it reads, "If your Advisor has sold you 36 annuities maybe its time for a new Advisor?"

To keep your car running efficiently, you need to get regular tune-ups, inflate the tires properly, change the oil on schedule, and more. It's not enough to just fill the tank. To get the most miles per gallon, you must attend to all the rest. Your Wealth Strategy is like your car. As we work on it together, we decide what needs attention first. Your engine may be idling rough, but if you have a flat tire, you won't be going anywhere.

You need the appropriate investments in the right balance, tailored to your situation and income needs. What do you care about the most? What are your most pressing needs and wants? We need to find that out and invest accordingly. That's how you keep the cash flowing.

QUESTIONS TO CONSIDER

- ♀ Have you created an income plan that determines when and how your income will be paid to you during retirement?

- ♀ Does your current retirement plan consider all five risk factors: inflation, taxes, market risk, health care costs, and legacy?

- ♀ Have you determined your income deficit?

- ♀ Do you believe you have sufficient diversification of your income sources?

A WORLD OF RISKS

Can you afford to make a mistake now?

On the final approach to retirement, the risks that threaten your dreams feel more urgent. You now have so very much to lose, and you must hold on to those hard-earned gains. Most people think of market risk as the primary concern. There are many other risks, however, such as inflation, fluctuating interest rates, taxes, and the cost of custodial care. The primary risk, ironically, is that we are enjoying longer, more active lives. We simply may outlive our money.

M y wife, Alexis, particularly loves Thanksgiving, because it is the one holiday when I do all the cooking, preparing the holiday dinner each year as described in the November issue of *Food & Wine* magazine. It has long been our tradition to celebrate with friends as well as family. Each year I begin the planning well in advance so I can make sure everything is perfect.

Twenty-five years ago, shortly after Alexis and I met, the holiday did not go so smoothly. I had just purchased a row house in the Mount Airy section of Philadelphia, and I wanted to have all my friends over for dinner. On the Saturday after the holiday, I invited about twenty people to my new house—including my girlfriend, whom, of course, I hoped to impress.

Not knowing what to serve, I bought a copy of *Food & Wine* magazine's Thanksgiving issue. I decided to prepare whatever meal had been published in that edition. After carefully reviewing the recipes, I put together my list and went shopping for a turkey and all the trimmings at Reading Terminal Market, the center city farmers' market, located in a cavernous hall that once was a railroad station. I bought a fresh bird at Godshall's Poultry. I got a bottle of champagne, which I was told was the best complement for turkey. I pored over the recipes in the magazine to get everything just right. As I worked, I cranked up the music, excited about the party to come.

After everyone had arrived and enjoyed a drink or two, the big moment came when we all sat down for the Thanksgiving feast. It was then that I discovered to my dismay that much of the turkey was still raw in the middle, even though I had been careful to cook it for the allotted time. I tried to stall by serving more appetizers and pouring a few more drinks, and finally I sliced off what was safely cooked and served the meal. But when people started asking for seconds, they were not to be had. My friend John got up to go into the kitchen for another slice, and his wife, Anne, quickly followed to head him off. She had already noticed the sorry state of the turkey. That's when I had to confess that the meat was still raw.

What had happened? I was at a loss to understand. I had planned so carefully. After everyone had left, as I sipped wine with my wife-to-be, she asked, "So, did you mean to leave the oven set to preheat?"

I had followed the recipe to the letter but didn't know how to operate the oven. Now, imagine that turkey representing your retirement account—everything you've saved for twenty or thirty years. You need to be equipped with whatever it takes to get the job done, or some unforeseen risk could mess up your party.

To this day, I still cook the Thanksgiving meal, and many of those friends who were at the first meal, including Anne and John, come back every year. I still do my shopping at Godshall's. These days, with a quarter century of experience, I can cook without a recipe. It's all about carefully preparing and following a proven routine. Now, though, I always buy two turkeys. One of them I cook the night before, making sure I've got the time and temperature right. That one provides the leftovers. I want to send everyone home with a delicious, safe meal.

UNDERSTANDING WHERE YOU ARE

It is impossible to make any type of intelligent decision about your future before thoroughly understanding both your past and your present. This always starts with looking at your relationship to money. What are your values? Who in your life is important to you? And most important, what is your vision for retirement?

I need to know about your personal concerns, your health issues, the quality of your relationships, whether you are responsible for supporting your children or a parent—all of these things and more define your current position.

Next, it's time to look at your assets. By the time many people come to me for assistance, they are nearing retirement and have already positioned their assets. Usually, those assets consist of a collection of stuff they have picked up along the way. They might have multiple 401(k)s or other employer retirement plans. They might have an investment record of, say, five years here and five years there as somebody new convinced them to take a different approach. Frankly, that is typical. If they already have a financial plan, they probably haven't paid much attention to it for a long time and want to know whether they're still on the right track.

Sometimes, when I ask if they have a retirement plan, I will get the response, "Sure, I have an IRA and a 401(k)." Please remember that just having a retirement savings account is not the same as having a retirement or financial plan.

Now we apply our process to determine how each risk factor could derail your dreams. For example, how will market volatility, inflation, fluctuating interest rates, taxes, and health care and long-term care costs influence your ability to achieve your goals? What might happen if your spouse suddenly dies or needs custodial care for a long period of time? We must identify which risks could have the greatest influence on the quality of your retirement.

With all that prep work done, it's time to dive deep into your current investments and other available financial resources to make your vision of retirement a reality.

THE ART OF INVESTING

When weighing the amount of risk in an investment, you should think of your expected rate of return as only a potential. If you see that an investment has returned an annual average of 7 percent over the last decade, you may be tempted to tell yourself that you will receive 7 percent over the next decade. Let me share an axiom that you no doubt have heard before: Past performance is no guarantee of future results.

In other words, you only know that you have the potential of making that 7 percent. You don't know whether you will actually get it. At a 7 percent average return, a million-dollar investment might return $70,000 next year, or it might not.

You must also consider the downside risk, which could be considerably greater than the potential for gain. Let's say the investment with the 7 percent average return has the potential to lose 25 percent of its value in any one year. In order to give your million dollars the potential of gaining $70,000 on average, you would have to accept the possibility of losing a quarter of your portfolio. This means your downside risk is $250,000 in any one year. In other words, that is how much you are willing to bet that you can average a $70,000 annual return. It's not that simple, though. You will want to know the odds of winning or losing. Do you have a 50/50 chance of hitting that annual average every year? Will you experience a major loss every five to seven years?

In essence, that's the art of investing. Every year you have a potential to make a certain amount and to lose a certain amount. Therefore, you need to know the upside potential, the downside risk, and the odds of winning. To evaluate an investment risk, you need to know all three.

"Just how much risk *can* I take?" people often ask me, and I tell them that it's important to look at market risk in three ways. I use the acronym **CAN** to describe those principal elements of risk. The letters stand for "capacity," "attitude," and "need." All too often, though, people think of risk only in terms of capacity. Let's look at each of these factors:

Capacity is the amount of risk you would be willing to take, with no other considerations. Most investment consultants will give you a risk questionnaire, seeking to determine your risk capacity. Are you an aggressive investor? Or are you a moderate investor, or a conservative one? The questionnaire is not asking about anything in your life other than your willingness to take risks. The consultant is concerned only about whether an investment is appropriate for the risk level that you have identified. The risk level you can tolerate may not be appropriate for your desired lifestyle. It may not fit your stage in life, but if you have indicated that you can accept that level of risk, that is all the consultant needs to know. You answer the questionnaire; the consultant determines that you are, say, a moderate investor; and you get stuck on the pie chart for moderate risk takers.

Think of risk capacity this way: Imagine you are cruising across Pennsylvania on Interstate 80 in your Lexus. It's a beautiful day, the traffic is light, and no state troopers are out and about. You figure you can go as fast as you want, as if you were driving on the Autobahn. Before long, your speedometer registers 100 miles an hour. That's your capacity. That's how fast you will go when everything lines up for you. Others will stay at or below the speed limit; a few might even pass you. Each driver has his or her own capacity. And if anything changes—let's say a storm sweeps in—you might slow to fifty while others pull off to wait it out.

Likewise, investors each have their own capacity, and they should adjust for conditions. Not every day in the market will be sunny. The world changes, individual lives change, and people get in trouble when they fail to recognize that. That's why so many people lost so much when the dot-com bubble burst at the turn of the millennium and during the recession several years later. They may have thought that they were diversified, but in truth, they were driving at capacity and skidded out of control when the storm came.

If you are in retirement or on the verge of it, you simply don't have time to recover from such a skid. You can't depend on a risk tolerance questionnaire alone to determine the proper mix of your investments.

Attitude is the second element of the acronym. Our ability to harness emotions plays a big role in investment success. You might say you have the capacity to lose 15 percent in any given year and believe you would be just fine, but when you see your $500,000 dip to $425,000, will you be able to stick with your plan? As a human being, you likely will feel quite a few reservations. Your attitude toward risk will change, despite your expressed capacity for risk. Attitude changes behavior, and behavior determines results.

Let's look at this another way. Instead of using the word attitude, let's use risk perception. You may have a risk capacity of being able to lose 15 percent of your assets without being concerned or panicking. But if your risk perception is that the loss of 15 percent is just the beginning of a bigger correction, this can lead to wildly inappropriate investment decisions.

Need describes how much risk you need to take to achieve your personal and financial goals. How much money do you need to make? As you approach retirement, what level of risk will be required to achieve your goals? Perhaps you will not need to take any risk, because your resources are sufficient for a lifetime. Perhaps you will want to take on a considerable amount of risk, because you have a lot to make up. That's why it is essential to determine just how much you will need to make in order to realize your vision of retirement. Matching your requirements to your resources is the sensible way to put a portfolio together.

Remember, your money needs to last for the rest of your life, so you need to consider all three elements of risk in your strategy.

PRESERVATION, INCOME, AND GROWTH

There are three important concepts you need to keep top of mind when creating an investment strategy. Preservation of capital, generating income, and allocating for growth are very different types of investment strategies and can use very different types of investment vehicles. All three are important to a smart investment strategy, but how you balance the three will change over time.

If you remember earlier in the book, we discussed the difference between building a retirement nest egg and having a retirement nest egg. During your accumulation years, you were building your retirement nest egg, which meant you were focused on growth first, income second, and preservation of capital third. Because you had a long time horizon and didn't depend on your nest egg for income, you weren't worried about short-term fluctuations in your investments. Time and compounding of your returns was on your side.

But now you need your money to last for the rest of your life. You need your money to generate income for you for the rest of your life. Your priorities have changed. It is now more important than ever to preserve your capital for as long as possible, generate income in good times and bad, and grow your nest egg a little to protect against inflation.

Unfortunately, many advisors will ignore one of these strategies, at their clients' peril. Some advisors maintain that you should focus only on growth, and everything will be fine. It's as if they were wearing blinders back in 2008. Other advisors insist that only a guaranteed income such as an annuity is acceptable, but can that fixed income plan keep up with inflation? And even though that income will last the rest of your life, nothing will be left on the day you pass away. You will have income without preservation or growth.

VOLATILITY OF YOUR INVESTMENTS

The volatility of your investments refers to the size of the swing, or the wobble, in your investment returns. If you own a CD paying 1 percent, then you will be pretty sure that for every year you own that CD, you will receive a 1 percent return. A CD has practically no wobble.

If you invested in the S&P 500, its historical return (adjusted for inflation) is about 7 percent. But as we have seen over the last fifteen years, you could experience a double-digit loss in one year and a double-digit gain the next. This was not as much of a concern while you were accumulating your wealth as it is now that you have to live off your wealth for the rest of your life.

Understanding and managing the volatility of your investments is critical to having a financially successful retirement.

THE TWO BROTHERS

Tom and Jerry were twins. Each retired at age sixty-two with a portfolio of $1 million. Tom believed that the best way to invest was to buy the S&P 500 index and let it ride. Jerry was a little more concerned with the wild swings of the market and decided to invest in a portfolio that was less volatile. It had less wobble.

Both brothers needed to take out $40,000 a year from their investments. As you can see from the following tables, Tom ended up with $694,393 and Jerry ended up with $1,528,669. Both portfolios had the same arithmetic average return over a fifteen-year period. So what happened? Volatility.

Year	Portfolio 1	Beg Bal	Earnings	Withdrawal	End Bal
2000	-9.06%	$1,000,000	-$90,600	-$40,000	$869,400
2001	-12.02%	$869,400	-$104,502	-$40,000	$724,898
2002	-22.15%	$724,898	-$160,565	-$40,000	$524,333
2003	28.50%	$524,333	$149,435	-$40,000	$633,768
2004	10.74%	$633,768	$68,067	-$40,000	$661,835
2005	4.77%	$661,835	$31,570	-$40,000	$653,404
2006	15.64%	$653,404	$102,192	-$40,000	$715,597
2007	5.39%	$715,597	$38,571	-$40,000	$714,167
2008	-37.02%	$714,167	-$264,385	-$40,000	$409,783
2009	26.49%	$409,783	$108,551	-$40,000	$478,334
2010	14.91%	$478,334	$71,320	-$40,000	$509,654
2011	1.97%	$509,654	$10,040	-$40,000	$479,694
2012	15.82%	$479,694	$75,888	-$40,000	$515,581
2013	32.18%	$515,581	$165,914	-$40,000	$641,496
2014	13.51%	$641,496	$86,666	-$40,000	$688,162
2015	1.25%	$688,162	$8,602	-$40,000	$656,764
2016	11.82%	$656,764	$77,629	-$40,000	$694,393
Average	6.04%				
Std Dev	18.08%				

DISCLAIMER: The above table is intended to illustrate the potential results of a hypothetical investment of $1,000,000 in the Vanguard 500 Index Inv (VFINX) beginning on the first trading day of 2000 and held through the last trading day of 2016, with $50,000 withdrawn from the investment on an annual basis. It is assumed that any dividends and other earnings are reinvested and no allowances for external advisory fees have been made. The results may vary significantly if the beginning day/and or the ending day is altered. The holdings comprising the fund have changed over time and are likely to change in the future. The fund performance and other information was acquired from Morningstar Direct. It is believed to be accurate but has not been independently verified by TFG Wealth Management LLC. Past performance is not necessarily indicative of future results.

Year	Portfolio 2	Beg Bal	Earnings	Withdrawal	End Bal
2000	3.83%	$1,000,000	$38,275	-$40,000	$998,275
2001	-0.03%	$998,275	-$250	-$40,000	$958,025
2002	0.18%	$958,025	$1,693	-$40,000	$919,718
2003	18.57%	$919,718	$170,747	-$40,000	$1,050,466
2004	9.23%	$1,050,466	$96,965	-$40,000	$1,107,430
2005	5.50%	$1,107,430	$60,953	-$40,000	$1,128,383
2006	10.70%	$1,128,383	$120,723	-$40,000	$1,209,107
2007	4.08%	$1,209,107	$49,292	-$40,000	$1,218,399
2008	-1.16%	$1,218,399	-$14,166	-$40,000	$1,164,232
2009	10.45%	$1,164,232	$121,661	-$40,000	$1,245,893
2010	8.20%	$1,245,893	$102,198	-$40,000	$1,308,091
2011	5.06%	$1,308,091	$66,226	-$40,000	$1,334,318
2012	8.07%	$1,334,318	$107,629	-$40,000	$1,401,946
2013	10.01%	$1,401,946	$140,325	-$40,000	$1,502,271
2014	7.81%	$1,502,271	$117,269	-$40,000	$1,579,540
2015	-1.74%	$1,579,540	-$27,411	-$40,000	$1,512,129
2016	3.74%	$1,512,129	$56,540	-$40,000	$1,528,669
Average	6.03%				
Std Dev	5.21%				

DISCLAIMER: The above table is intended to illustrate the potential results of a hypothetical investment of $1,000,000, with $50,000 withdrawn from the investment on an annual basis, in a hypothetical mix of securities, which would yield a series of returns that are less volatile than the returns of an investment intended to track the S&P five hundred over the same time period, beginning on the first trading day of 2000 and held through the last trading day of 2016. The table does not represent the results of an investment of an actual security or mix of securities.

Tom's portfolio returns ranged from a high of 28.50 percent to a low of −37.02 percent.

Jerry's portfolio returns ranged from a high of 18.57 percent to a low of -1.74 percent.

When Tom and Jerry made their initial investment, could they predict the results over the next fifteen years? Of course not. They didn't have a crystal ball, of course.

But what Tom and Jerry could have known was the wobble, or volatility, of each of their portfolios .

Keep in mind that when investing for retirement, you want to put yourself in a position to have a positive outcome regardless of the ups and downs of your investments.

So why did Tom end up with so much less than Jerry? It was the result of an investment phenomenon called *reverse dollar cost averaging*.

Reverse dollar cost averaging is the opposite side of the coin from *dollar cost averaging*, which is a common strategy when saving for retirement. With dollar cost averaging, you save a set amount of money on a regular basis over many years. This takes the guessing out of timing your investment purchases. The goal is to purchase your investments at their average price over a long period of time.

Reverse dollar cost averaging happens when you withdraw a fixed amount out of your accounts over a long period of time. The problem with this strategy is that it makes the years when you have a negative performance even worse and the years you have a positive performance much less positive than expected.

Take a look at what happened to Tom and Jerry's portfolios in a down year and an up year.

REBALANCING

Once you have determined your approach to investing, it's time to monitor and manage your portfolio. You don't make money until you sell something. If you never sell anything, the value in your account can be high or low or anywhere in between. It doesn't matter until you cash it in, so clearly you need a disciplined approach to selling, which is called a *sell discipline*. To truly buy at the bottom and sell at the top is a rarity, but you want to aim for that ideal.

Investors generally feel reluctant to sell while their stock values are rising, because they don't want to lose out on all the potential they see. They hold on tight until the value peaks and starts to fall again. That's human nature, but it costs them money.

An asset allocation plan, built on the foundation of a comprehensive Wealth Strategy, forces investors to be disciplined with their investments. One of the roles of a financial advisor is to help families invest objectively and rationally. To that end, the investments within a portfolio need to be rebalanced regularly. If one investment is doing very well, it eventually can get out of bounds and claim an ever-larger portion of the overall portfolio. Your original aim may have been to keep 20 percent in that investment, but now you find it represents 30 percent. You are pleased with that gain, and it's hard to say goodbye to a winner. But then again, if you never sell it, you never make money on it.

Remember that what goes up must come down in the investment world, and what is down may very well be ready to rise again. You will be better off with a rebalancing approach that systematically harvests some of your successes so you can buy more of your weaker players. Why would you put more into securities that are hurting? Because you believe in them. Otherwise, why would you even own them? Why would they be in your portfolio? If you are confident that an investment will be making you money over the long haul, then the perfect time to buy is when it's down. If you don't feel that way, then get rid of it.

Do you agree that the proven formula for making money is to buy low and to sell high? If so, the rebalancing approach to asset allocation will work for you over time if you have properly chosen your allocation and underlying investments. Asset allocation, not individual stock picking, is the primary means by which wise investors boost their returns.

Some investors think of rebalancing as abiding by the "Rule of 100," a basic formula for asset allocation that was advanced by John Bogle, founder of the Vanguard Group. The rule maintains that you should subtract your age from 100, with the result being the percentage of your portfolio that you could reasonably expose to risky investments. The remainder of your portfolio, according to the rule, should be in relatively conservative investments. As you get older, in other words, the Rule of 100 calls for regularly rebalancing your portfolio to make it progressively less risky.

That conversation is strictly about risk capacity. Individual investors might have a good reason to be more conservative than the Rule of 100 would suggest for them. Whether the rule makes sense at any given time also depends on economic and political conditions at home and abroad. There are times to be even more conservative than the rule would suggest, and there are times when it might be wise to pursue more aggressive opportunities.

Certainly, the world is far different than when Bogle devised that rule. Back then, the prevailing wisdom was that bond funds were low risk, and the approach was interpreted as "invest your age in bonds." With interest rates at historic lows and likely to rise, bonds represent a much greater risk than in years past, and yet many people still design their portfolio in a basic stock/bond Rule of 100 asset allocation.

INVESTMENT EXPENSES

In my grandfather's later years, after my grandmother passed away, I had dinner with him at least one night a week at his apartment in the Philadelphia suburb of Glenside. We would talk about family, current events, and my new career in the financial services business. He often pointed out that there's a cost to everything and when you buy an investment or anything else, you need to weigh the cost versus the benefit or value. The problem, he said, is you often don't know the true cost—and whenever anyone tries to tell you it won't cost anything, be very cautious.

"There's no free lunch," my grandfather warned me. His observation comes to mind when I think about the expenses involved in mutual funds, the most common investment vehicle in our country today.

Mutual funds do have a place in the investment world, but I must emphasize they aren't the best option for all investors. Although mutual funds have long made up a large part of retirement savings, few people understand how the fees and expenses within those funds can drain away their dollars. Early in my career, when I helped start Stone Bridge Mutual Funds, I learned about how mutual funds had become a money-making machine for large financial institutions.

Open-end mutual funds, introduced in 1924, opened a world of opportunities for small investors who could gain access to professional portfolio management and diversify by buying into a fund. In 1929, just before the stock market crash, nineteen mutual funds existed. Today there are thousands—far more than the number of companies that trade on the New York Stock Exchange—and most of that growth has taken place over the past twenty years. About half of all US households have investments in mutual funds. Small investors can find a fund that specializes in just about any asset class:

stocks, bonds, commodities, real estate, currencies, art, precious metals, and more.

The investor isn't the only one with the potential for profit. The brokers who sell shares of mutual funds get generous commissions. The companies that create the funds charge fees to manage and administer them. They almost always make money from mutual funds. For the investors, unfortunately, that isn't always the case.

Mutual funds support a huge industry, and everyone wants a cut. The industry includes, for example, custodians that hold the funds, sales and wholesaling organizations that distribute and market the funds, law firms that specialize in mutual funds, accounting and reporting firms, rating services, and mutual fund newsletters. The profits support hundreds of thousands of jobs.

Investors and regulators have been taking a hard look at what goes on behind the scenes. The expenses can be much higher than you might think. They include expenses that are stated and those that are unstated. The stated expenses are spelled out in the fund prospectus, which lists the expense ratio. The average ratio, according to the Investment Company Institute, is 1.4 percent per year. The unstated expenses are harder to quantify, but they may total considerably more than that. Let's look at some of those unstated expenses.

Trading costs—Known in the industry as the *bid/offer spread*, trading costs are part of the internal workings of each fund. Whenever a manager buys and sells securities, the fund incurs costs. When there is a lot of trading, those expenses mount. They can add a percentage point or two to the total cost for investors.

Transaction commissions—The processing of any trade order incurs a cost. Even with a low commission structure, the costs can't be avoided, and again, the impact on investors is greater when the fund trades more actively.

Market impact costs—When funds execute large trades, the sheer size of the transaction can move the price of a security higher or lower. If the manager sells, for example, 200,000 shares, the stock price could drop significantly. In other words, the trading itself changes the price of the asset, and that slippage represents a cost for the investor.

Mutual funds don't report those types of trading expenses (mainly because they're difficult to calculate), but professional estimates put the figure at 1 to 3 percent annually for equity mutual funds. That's a major drain on retirement savings. A $250,000 nest egg, for example, earning 5 percent over fifteen years would grow to about $520,000. If just 1 percentage point is sacrificed to fees, it would only grow to $450,000. If fees claim 3 percentage points, the result is about $336,000.

As you can see, fund expenses drastically reduce the compounding effect, and that impact gets even more painful when you begin withdrawing from your account. As the nest egg shrinks, you will need an increasingly larger percentage of distributions to maintain the same lifestyle. Every dollar of expense that a mutual fund incurs is a dollar you don't keep. Remember, the prospectus only reveals some of those expenses. When you add up the stated and the unstated costs, the burden can be more than you would want to bear.

Fees are what keep the system operating, and we must remember that there is no free lunch—but then again, you don't want to overpay. That's the problem with the so-called "hidden fees" that are part of the mutual fund world. Investors overpay because they can't see what is happening. The remedy for this is as much transparency as possible.

Please don't assume I'm against all investments in mutual funds or any other type of investment product. My point here is to be aware of both the obvious costs and potential hidden costs of any investment, because whether it is a mutual fund, an annuity, or a managed account, what is most important is that you get value for your money. The cheapest investment vehicle isn't always the best, but neither is the most expensive. Remember that in the investment world, there is much more than the rate of return that produces value for you and your wealth.

INTEREST RATE RISK

The Federal Reserve regularly adjusts the prevailing interest rates as it keeps a finger on the economic pulse. To keep inflation down, for example, it may raise interest rates in an attempt to cool the economy. Conversely, the Fed may lower interest rates if it perceives the need to stimulate spending and ward off a recession. It may take action several times in relatively quick succession, or it may make no changes for many months.

As history has shown, this is an inexact science. Economists can see trends, but nobody has a crystal ball to predict interest rates, just as no one knows for sure the course of the stock market. That presents yet another significant risk that you must recognize. If you're basing your income hopes on an expected interest rate, be careful: that might not be the rate you get.

A certificate of deposit paid interest of several percent not that long ago, and back in the 1970s and 1980s, in the days of double digit inflation, CDs yields were double digit as well. Even at a return of 5 percent, you might have felt comfortable with the $50,000 a year you would get from a million-dollar investment. What would you do, though, when those CDs matured? Could you reinvest and live on the $10,000 a year from the recent, meager rates of perhaps 1 percent?

That's a simple example of interest rate risk, which can hurt investors when they can't continue to command the kind of returns that will support their lifestyle. The question you need to ask yourself is, will your interest-rate-sensitive investment be a reliable source of income during your retirement? If not, what are you going to do about it? There are a number of strategies we use to deal with this type of risk, but the best approach depends on your income needs and which strategy makes the most sense for you.

THE EFFECT OF MARKET INTEREST RATES ON BOND PRICES AND YIELD

A second concern that bond investors in particular need to pay close attention to is the impact a change in interest rates can have on the value of bonds, bond mutual funds, and bond exchange-traded funds (ETFs) you may own. Consider the following example from the SEC investor bulletin "Interest Rate Risk—When Interest Rates Go Up, Prices of Fixed Rate Bonds Fall."

A fundamental principle of bond investing is that market interest rates and bond prices generally move in opposite directions. When market interest rates rise, prices of fixed-rate bonds fall. This phenomenon is known as interest rate risk.

A seesaw, such as the one pictured below, can help you visualize the relationship between market interest rates and bond prices. Imagine that one end of the seesaw represents the market interest rate and the other end represents the price of a fixed-rate bond.

MARKET INTEREST RATES AND PRICES OF FIXED-RATE BONDS MOVE IN OPPOSITE DIRECTIONS

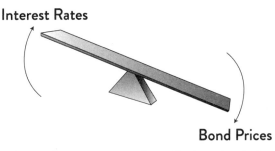

Interest Rates

Bond Prices

Higher market interest rates = lower fixed-rate bond prices
Lower market interest rates = higher fixed-rate bond prices

A bond's yield to maturity shows how much an investor's money will earn if the bond is held until it matures. For example, as the table below illustrates, let's say a Treasury bond offers a 3% coupon rate, and a year later market interest rates fall to 2%. The bond will still pay a 3% coupon rate, making it more valuable than new bonds paying just a 2% coupon rate. If you sell the 3% bond before it matures, you will probably find that its price is higher than it was a year ago. Along with the rise in price, however, the yield to maturity of the bond will go down for anyone who buys the bond at the new higher price.

EXAMPLE 1: IF MARKET INTEREST RATES DECREASE BY ONE PERCENT

Financial Term	Today	One Year Later
Market Interest Rate	3%	2%
Coupon Rate (semi-annual payments)	3%	3%
Face Value	$1,000	$1,000
Maturity	10 years	9 years remaining
Price	$1,000	$1,082
Yield to Maturity	3%	2%

Now suppose market interest rates rise from 3% to 4%, as the table below illustrates. If you sell the 3% bond, it will be competing with new Treasury bonds that offer a 4% coupon rate. The price of the 3% bond may be more likely to fall. The yield to maturity, however, will rise as the price falls.[5]

EXAMPLE 2: IF MARKET INTEREST RATES INCREASE BY ONE PERCENT

Financial Term	Today	One Year Later
Market Interest Rate	3%	2%
Coupon Rate (semi-annual payments)	3%	3%
Face Value	$1,000	$1,000
Maturity	10 years	9 years remaining
Price	$1,000	$925
Yield to Maturity	3%	4%

Higher market interest rates = lower fixed-rate bond prices = higher fixed-rate bond yields

Generally, interest rates have been falling since the mid-1980s to historic lows. Bond prices have been steadily increasing over the same period of time. Investors need to consider when the seesaw is likely

5 "Interest Rate Risk—When Interest Rates Go Up, Prices of Fixed Rate Bonds Fall," SEC Pub. No/ 151 (6/13) Office of Investor Education and Advocacy: Investor Bulletin:

to rock the other way. What will happen to the value of your bonds, or worse, your bond mutual funds?

Because we have been in a bull bond market for the last thirty years, most investors have become very comfortable owning bonds inside a bond mutual fund. Because interest rates have steadily gone down, the value of many of these funds has increased over time well above the interest they produce. But you have to ask yourself, when interest rates start going back up, what will happen to the value of my bond mutual fund? It will probably start losing value.

In a rising interest rate environment, you could lose a lot of money in bond funds. This doesn't mean you should abandon bonds in your portfolio, but you have to be smart about it.

OUR OWN WORST ENEMY

Since the way to make money in the market, simply enough, is to buy low and to sell high, why do so many investors end up doing just the opposite?

The fault is in us. The markets operate in cycles of gain and loss that reflect the human nature of the countless investors at work. When markets are on the rise, many investors feel optimistic about the prospect of gaining more and more. They are romping in a bull market, motivated by greed. And then, at the peak of their euphoria, they see their holdings start to slip. The investors are reluctant to believe it's happening, and they hold on tight for the downhill ride. They become fearful and may sell at the worst time.

Investment decisions based on emotions tend to be poor ones. Investors often feel compelled to rid themselves of their weak performers so they can buy more of those that have been surging ahead. As a result, they pay dearly for overpriced securities, and they don't see the underpriced bargains.

Setting your emotions aside

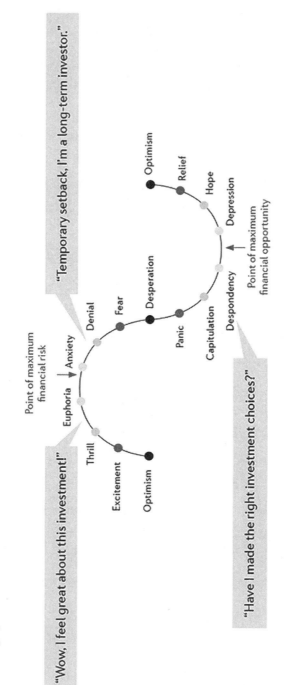

"Wow, I feel great about this investment!"

"Temporary setback, I'm a long-term investor."

"Have I made the right investment choices?"

Optimism

Excitement

Thrill

Euphoria

Anxiety

← Point of maximum financial risk

Denial

Fear

Desperation

Panic

Capitulation

Despondency

Depression

Point of maximum financial opportunity →

Hope

Relief

Optimism

Much has been written about the various biases and behavioral tendencies that play into investors' decision-making. For example, investors tend to think that what has been happening in the market is what will continue to happen. They tend to follow the crowd, as if part of a herd, running with the bull and running from the bear, favoring the investments that others are choosing. They seek out information and opinions that bolster their preconceived views and ignore anyone who will dampen their enthusiasm.

In its latest report on investor behavior, the investment research firm Dalbar found that in 2015, the average investor in equity mutual funds underperformed the S&P 500 by a margin of 3.66 percent.[6] Over twenty years, the average investor got an annualized return of only 4.67 percent compared to the S&P annualized return for the period of 8.19 percent—a difference of 3.52 percent. Dalbar's annual reports have consistently shown this poor performance. What do those investors do wrong? Dalbar attributes the gap to their tendency to chase returns.

Each of us holds a worldview that also will play into investment decisions. Some people's pessimism leads them to avoid as much risk as possible—and miss opportunities. Those with abounding optimism may take too much risk and fail to take a protective stance when appropriate. Neither optimism nor pessimism will serve your best interests. The best investors take an impartial and rational approach, free of emotion and personal biases. We need to become aware of the human emotion that can lead us astray so we can gain the proper perspective needed for wise investment decisions. Otherwise, the biggest risk we face very well might be ourselves.

---

6 "Dalbar's 22nd Annual Quantitative Analysis of Investor Behavior," Dalbar, Inc. (2016). http://www.qidllc.com/wp-content/uploads/2016/02/2016-Dalbar-QAIB-Report.pdf.

While many families seek out financial advisors for their expertise in financial planning or investment strategy, a lot of the work that we do is to keep our clients from making emotional decisions about what to do with their investments. If, in 2007, just before the crash, you were told to sell out all your investments, would you? In March of 2009, if you were told to jump back into the market with both feet, would you?

QUESTIONS TO CONSIDER

- Do you know how much volatility/risk is in your investments?
- Has anyone ever discussed this with you?
- Do you think this important to know?
- Have you evaluated your current financial situation in terms of the different risks you will face in retirement?
- If you are working with a financial professional, are you working with a product salesman, an investment consultant, or a wealth manager?
- Have you evaluated how market volatility will affect your retirement income?
- Have you rebalanced your investments in the last year?
- Are you aware of all the fees you are paying, hidden or disclosed?
- How much interest rate risk do you have in your portfolio?
- Do you make decisions about your investments based on emotion or based on facts?
- Have you determined your risk capacity, attitude, and necessary "minimum retirement rate of return"?

Chapter 7

TAX SENSE

Will you get blindsided by taxes?

Taxation is one of the largest expenses in retirement and must be carefully managed to avoid huge losses over the years. Tax issues have become increasingly important in this era, where most people have their savings in tax-deferred retirement plans. The government wants its cut.

T ony the homeowner notices some shingles in the yard after a storm and, looking up, realizes it's time for a new roof. He has some contractors take a look and settles on a bid for $22,000. Tony figures he can get that money from his

IRA, so he calls to get a check for that amount. The next month, he's surprised to see a $28,000 distribution on his statement.

You may be more sophisticated than Tony in your understanding of the workings of IRAs, 401(k)s, and other tax-deferred accounts. I can tell you it isn't unusual for people to be stunned by the amount of taxes they must pay on their withdrawals. The money in these accounts has grown for years, sheltered from taxation, and Uncle Sam now wants his cut.

Today most retirees have a large part of their savings in tax-deferred accounts. As they watched that money grow over time, they also created for themselves a huge tax liability—and they can't truly know the extent of that liability for years. As history has shown us, we can't predict the tax rates that we will be facing, whether in a year or two or in twenty years.

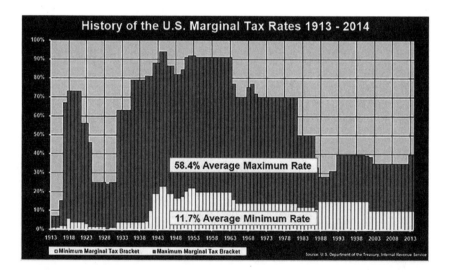

Most retirees don't realize that their tax liability can have major implications on their retirement standard of living. A retiree may be excited to observe that his 401(k) has grown to $1 million. "If I take out just 4 percent a year," he says, "I'll have $40,000 on top of my

Social Security and be doing just fine!" What he doesn't realize is that he doesn't have a million dollars. A quarter of that, potentially, isn't his. The government owns it. The tax bill is coming due.

In this chapter, we will briefly look at how you can greatly benefit from proper tax management. Please keep in mind that there are many books dedicated to this subject. Every year, I sit down with tax experts who share dozens of strategies to reduce taxes on retirement accounts and retirement income. But as we all know, taxes and the tax code are constantly changing, and so do the strategies we need to use to minimize our annual tax bill.

Taxation will be one of your largest expenses in retirement. You need to plan carefully for how you will handle it, and the sooner the better. The longer you defer taxes in a retirement account, the larger the tax bill will grow. Unless you develop a strategy for dealing with that situation, you, your spouse, and your heirs could face a huge expense.

We all owe our fair share of taxes, of course, but the operative word there is "fair." Every year, Americans hand over a fortune in taxes that they need not have paid if they had pursued wiser strategies. Generally, it isn't some big blunder that drains the money away. Rather, the money leaks from their portfolios in drips, year after year. This is money that might otherwise have compounded to push their savings to much greater heights. The opportunity cost is staggering.

TAX DIVERSITY

From a tax perspective, you are likely to have assets of three fundamental types in your portfolio: taxable, tax-deferred, and tax-free. In other words, some of your assets will be subject to immediate taxation; some will be taxed in the future; and some never will be taxed. In a well-designed portfolio, each of those tax treatments will play an important role.

As you plan your income for retirement, you will want to find the right balance so that you pay no more than necessary in taxes. All three types of accounts have a place and a purpose. If you use them improperly, you could end up surrendering a sizable portion of your portfolio to the government. On the other hand, you can greatly benefit from a strategy that uses the three types wisely and positions them properly. Tax diversification is an essential element of effective financial planning. Your portfolio needs to be diversified for taxes, just as it needs to be diversified among investments.

Let's look at how these three "tax buckets" can provide tax diversity. Please keep in mind that there are actually more buckets, with different degrees of tax treatment, but these are the principal three.

Remember, your strategy should maximize the amount of income available for your use while also limiting the amount of income that you must declare on your tax return. By withdrawing from the appropriate buckets in the right blend, you can enjoy a significant income while shielding much of it from taxation.

TAXABLE INVESTMENTS

Investments held in taxable accounts are those on which you must pay income tax for the year that they produce earnings. These accounts can hold a broad category of assets that include stocks, ETFs, Treasury and corporate bonds, certificates of deposit, and mutual funds, to name a few.

You need to be particularly careful with mutual funds. They can generate what is known as phantom income tax. Let's say a fund manager buys a stock at $50 a share in 2000, and it increases to

$100 a share by 2016. You buy into the fund in 2016, after most of that appreciation, so you don't see any of the gain personally. However, if the manager decides to sell that position, the gain of $50 must be distributed on a per share basis to all shareholders, and that includes you. You will have to pay even though you were late to the party. In fact, the overall fund value could drop, and you could see a loss for the year, yet you would still owe the tax on the gain of the security that was sold. Though it's called a phantom tax, the tax bill is quite real. If you are buying mutual funds outside of a tax-deferred account, you and your advisor must be alert to that potential.

TAX-FREE INVESTMENTS

Tax-free accounts and tax-free investments can grow without incurring a tax bill. They include municipal bonds, Roth IRAs, 529 education accounts, and certain insurance products. The interest income derived from bonds issued by cities, towns, schools, and other governmental entities generally isn't taxed at either the state or federal level. The Roth IRA is a retirement account to which you contribute after-tax dollars. All the gains created by the investments held in this account will never be taxed as long as you follow the rules. You can withdraw your money from a Roth without facing further taxes, neither on the amount that you contributed nor on the amount that it has grown. Likewise, a 529 account is also funded with after-tax dollars, and your withdrawals will be free of tax as long as you are using the money for qualified educational expenses. A properly structured life insurance policy, funded with after-tax money over the years, can grow to produce a cash value that could be tapped as nontaxable income—again, as long as you follow the rules.

TAX-DEFERRED INVESTMENTS

These include investments held within 401(k)-type retirement plans, 403(b) plans, traditional IRAs, and tax-deferred annuities, to name a few. Employee contributions are not immediately subject to income tax; instead, the government waits for its share until the account holder begins withdrawals, presumably during retirement. At that point, taxes will be due on both the contributions and the amount that they have grown. (Some employers do offer 401(k) plans with a Roth option, allowing participants to contribute after-tax money that they later can withdraw, tax-free.)

IRAs function similarly, but individuals can open them separately from their employers, and it's the government, not the employer, that sets the contribution limits. As with a 401(k) plan, the IRA account holder contributes pretax money. This can be done through either regular contributions or as an annual lump sum.

Tax-deferred annuities also offer the opportunity to postpone income tax until the time of distribution. They come in many forms, but essentially you can contribute money after it's taxed but pay no further tax on it as it grows. When it comes time for withdrawal, however, the IRS requires you pay tax on the portion of the annuity that represents your interest or growth—but not on your principal.

Again, the right balance among those types of investments is essential in producing the best cash flow for retirement. Unfortunately, as the 401(k)-type plans have proliferated, most people's retirement savings are heavily weighted toward tax-deferred investments, and they face a major tax bill in retirement. They lack the tax diversity required for a well-managed income plan.

In the days before the 401(k), previous generations used municipal bonds to produce tax-free income on top of their pensions and Social Security benefits. It was fairly straightforward. But with the advent of tax-deferred accounts, the strategies have become more complicated. In this post-pension age, not only are you expected to manage your own investment choices but you are also expected to figure out the best way to handle those tax buckets. It can be a heavy load.

THE 401(k) TAX TRAP

I'm sure you have heard the message that has been drilled into the ears of those who invest in 401(k)s, IRAs, and similar deferred-tax plans: "In retirement, you will be in a lower tax bracket. Get your deduction now, and pay a lower rate later in life. You will be set for life."

This line of reasoning has a couple of problems.

For one thing, the people who told you this ignored the fact that inflation can easily double the cost of living during retirement. This means you will need a lot more income just to maintain your desired lifestyle. In other words, your income will be higher because you need more money to live on which means you could be in a higher tax bracket.

Another concern is what is known as your required minimum distribution. After you reach seventy and a half, the government requires you to pay taxes on a portion of your tax deferred savings whether you need the money or not. This amount increases annually. If you don't take it out for any reason you will be assessed an astonishing 50 percent penalty, and of course you still will have to pay your ordinary income tax.

As an example, let's say you have a $50,000 pension and $40,000 in Social Security benefits. You are comfortable on that income, but all of a sudden you are forced to withdraw say another $40,000 from your IRA that you have allowed to grow tax deferred for decades. The added income could well push you into a much higher tax bracket. Higher than you were expecting many years ago when you started saving for retirement.

From a tax perspective, I believe that tax deferred accounts have the potential to devastate your retirement plan. You see, every dollar that you withdraw from your IRA or 401(k) will be taxed at your highest tax rate. This additional income can have a ripple effect on Medicare and other costs that are based upon how much income you report on your tax return. Just to add insult to injury it could also cause you to pay more taxes on your Social Security benefit.

In addition, these accounts are the highest-taxed asset that you can leave to your surviving spouse. There is no step-up in the cost basis for investments inside qualified accounts. The money is 100 percent taxable, and you are forced to withdraw money even when you don't want or need it. For all those reasons, I tell people that these types of plans—whether a 401(k), IRA, 403(b), or similar flavor— are a tax trap that they must start to deal with as early as possible, and well before age seventy-and-a-half, if possible.

Today's tax rates are at historic lows. For individuals, the top federal income tax rate currently is 39.6 percent. It was 70 percent back in the 1970s. At times in the 1940s and 1950s, it exceeded 90 percent. Historic lows tend to revert to historic averages or higher. With our nation facing political and economic pressures plus trillions in debt, the risk of taxes rising in the future are fairly high.

What many of us were told was a lie. Retirees will probably not be in a lower tax bracket than during their working years. Instead, countless people will be deferring into a higher tax bracket at a higher rate.

You could argue that without a 401(k) or similar plan, many people might save little or nothing for retirement and have nothing to leave to their heirs. Certainly, saving regularly for retirement is an important discipline, and these retirement plans do help people to do that. They are a means of setting aside money to compound. In addition, the company often provides a matching amount, and that is free money. I always recommend participating in a 401(k) to the extent that the company will offer a match. That helps to offset the tax issue. Otherwise, those tax implications are so serious that the only conclusion is that there must be a better way to prepare for retirement.

If you do have IRA money that you will be leaving to the next generation, one way to help soften the tax blow is through what is known as a *stretch provision*. Rather than receiving the proceeds as a lump sum, your heirs can have the option of continuing the tax deferral over their lifetimes. Regulations now allow them to withdraw the inherited money gradually, in minimum distributions. If set up and executed properly, the account could continue to grow, and your heirs could eventually leave it to their own children through another stretch provision.

However, you can't mandate the stretch. Your son or daughter or other beneficiary still could choose to take part or all of the money as a lump sum to use as he or she wishes—after paying the outrageous tax bill, of course. If you don't want the proceeds of your life's work to be blown on a fancy sports car purchased at a premium, you will want to make your wishes known well in advance.

The fundamental problem with 401(k)-type plans is that you are at the mercy of the prevailing tax rates, which can change with the stroke of a pen. These accounts can lose money overnight. If Congress raises taxes, the value of all that money that you worked hard for decades to set aside goes down. Or it can happen if your spouse dies and you need to begin paying the rate of a single taxpayer—nearly 30 percent more than you paid when filing jointly as a married couple. What happens then? Do you increase your withdrawals to maintain your lifestyle? You can end up in a vicious cycle in which you are paying more and more in taxes as you spend down your account.

It's likely that nobody has given you this perspective. What you hear instead is, "Put your money away in an IRA or 401(k), and look at how much money we can save you!" You don't hear about the big tax bill coming your way when you retire. Remember, you need tax diversity as well as investment diversity. If you are dumping money into a 401(k) beyond the company match, it's time to consider moving some of those resources into tax-free investments—a Roth, for example, or municipal bonds, or a life insurance policy. Or perhaps you should put money into a regular brokerage account so that you have more options upon retirement.

The bottom line is this: A tax plan is a critical part of an overall Wealth Strategy or retirement plan, whether you are among the super-rich or just middle class. Anyone who ignores this fact does so at his or her own peril. If your advisor is not talking to you about the tax implications of your investment strategy, are you really getting the best advice?

TAX-FREE INCOME FOR A SURVIVING SPOUSE

If a decent portion of your retirement income comes from IRAs, your tax burden might skyrocket after your spouse dies.

When a couple files their tax return jointly, this provides them with some of the most lenient treatment in the tax code. If one of them were to pass away, the surviving spouse would not be able to continue that status. The survivor would have to file as a single taxpayer, which is one of the harshest tax situations.

During retirement, most of a family's income is from retirement plans. IRAs and other retirement vehicles, like 401(k)s and 403(b)s, can cause significant tax challenges for surviving spouses.

So, what should you do about it? First, you need to find out what your tax return might look like for the surviving spouse. If you find out that you will be facing this problem, the good news is that there is a simple fix.

You can withdraw some extra income out of your IRA or other retirement plan today, and each year hence, while you and your spouse are both alive and enjoying lower taxes. If you do this, your tax burden while you are both alive will be higher, but that additional tax won't really affect your current lifestyle.

Then, take the after-tax amount of the distribution each year and use it to fund a life insurance policy on both your life and the life of your spouse. True, life insurance is more expensive for older folks, but surprisingly, due to increasing life expectancies, life insurance pricing has dropped considerably in recent years. As a result, this type of planning can be highly effective.

When the first spouse passes away, the surviving spouse will receive a big tax-free check from the life insurance company. He or she can use that check to convert the traditional IRAs to Roth IRAs. A Roth conversion requires you to pay tax on the appreciation of the assets in your retirement account. The survivor pays the tax from the life insurance proceeds.

As a result, all of the income that the Roth IRAs generate after that will be 100 percent tax-free. Another alternative is to pull some additional income from the life insurance proceeds. The surviving spouse can even give the tax-toxic traditional IRA money to the kids and live off of the life insurance proceeds, if the policy is large enough.

Adding a large tax-free check to the surviving spouse's list of assets can make a huge difference. He or she will be able to enjoy a comfortable income without the burden of the much higher rate for single taxpayers.

During my workshops, I share this story to highlight why preparing for the death of a spouse from a tax perspective is a very real issue.

SADIE'S SECRET

Murray and Sadie retired to Florida at age sixty-two. One day a decade later, Murray came home from the golf course and asked, "Sadie, will you remarry after I pass away?"

To which Sadie said, "Of course."

Murray, looking a little upset, asked, "Sadie, will you let him drive my brand-new, beautiful Cadillac?"

To which Sadie said, "Of course."

Murray, now more than a little flustered, asked, "Sadie, will you let him sit in my favorite spot on the couch on Sundays to watch the Eagles game?"

To which Sadie said, "Of course."

Now visibly agitated, Murray asked the most important question, "Sadie, will you let him use my favorite set of golf clubs?"

To which Sadie replied, "Of course not. He's left-handed."

Sadie clearly has her reasons for remarrying, and it seems she has more on her mind than saving on taxes once Murray was out of the picture. That's something she probably never even thought about, but it's certainly an incentive not to be single.

When your spouse dies in retirement, a few things happen. Besides losing one of your Social Security checks, you no longer can file your taxes jointly. You become a single tax filer, and that can devastate your retirement plan. Your tax costs can go up by 20 or 30 percent, or more. That translates to a lot less income. You need to deal with the risk that you or your spouse will become single again, dramatically changing his or her life—and tax situation. It's another of the many considerations a proper retirement plan or Wealth Strategy should include.

A MATTER OF PRIORITIES

"What is the best thing that we can do for our kids?" couples regularly ask me. I often suggest that opening a Roth IRA for them and contributing to it would be their best move. It's a way to leave them a tax-free gift that has the potential to grow exponentially by the time they receive it.

Another option is cash value life insurance. When properly structured, a permanent life insurance policy can provide tax-free dollars for your children in the future. When my children, Steven and Carly, were about ten years old, I purchased a permanent life insurance policy for each of them. I put away $75 a month for each policy. I expect by the time they are thirty years old, there should be tens of thousands of dollars in each policy for them. If they don't touch it until retirement, they could have hundreds of thousands of dollars to use, tax-free.

What you should do, of course, will depend upon your circumstances. As you manage your taxes, you must consider 1) the impact on you and your spouse while you are both alive; 2) the impact on the surviving spouse when one of you passes away; and 3) the impact on your children or other heirs when you leave them money. What you care about most is what will determine your strategies. You might want to begin an incremental conversion from your traditional IRA to a Roth IRA to provide that tax-free pool. Or you might purchase life insurance in a traditional estate tax strategy to greatly leverage the amount you can leave your heirs.

It's not a question of whether you are going to pay taxes. The question is, how can you rally a variety of strategies to make the most of your money while limiting the taxation? There is no one prescription. With so many variables, one size will never fit all. The best approach will depend upon family dynamics, needs, and wishes. It's a matter of priorities.

I've met people who don't seem to care how much they or their heirs will pay in taxes. That's their prerogative, I suppose, but they are a rarity. If instead you want more of your money to stay with your loved ones, much can be done. The IRS code is filled with opportunities to reduce taxes. It's in the government's interest to provide tax breaks for things that society wishes to promote, such as home ownership or charitable giving. And it's in your interest to steer clear of investments that could have severe tax consequences.

Recognizing that taxes are such a big issue when planning for retirement, we retain tax experts to help us craft strategies for the families we work with. We require our clients to send us their tax return every year, because we feel it is vitally important to managing our clients' financial plans. If your advisor has never asked to see your tax return, you need to ask yourself if you are getting the best advice possible.

QUESTIONS TO CONSIDER

- Why is it important to have "tax diversification" as well as diversified investments?
- What are the three principal tax "buckets?"
- What kind of investments should be in each of those buckets?
- How much do you have in each of them?

- 📍 How can a 401(k) plan or other deferred-tax account become a tax trap?
- 📍 What could be the best way to set aside money for your children?
- 📍 If your spouse dies, are you ready for the tax consequences of filing single?

THE COST OF CARE

Do you have a long-term care plan?

As we live longer, the infirmities of age not only slow us down but also can become highly expensive. A major threat to the retirement portfolio is the potential that you or your spouse may need long-term care. Careful planning can avoid these devastating costs.

"How many people have a long-term care plan?" I often ask my audience during workshops. At one of those discussions, a woman named Elizabeth raised her hand to explain that her daughter-in-law was a nurse. Elizabeth said that if she or her husband were to become ill, they would just move in with her son and daughter-in-law. "She'll take care of us."

I listened, nodded, and acknowledged that some families have taken that approach, especially in previous generations. "So, Elizabeth, have you told your daughter-in-law this?" I asked her. Her response: "Not yet."

Elizabeth's "plan," frankly, isn't all that unusual. Many families still aspire to take care of their own. In an earlier day, in fact, before the proliferation of nursing homes and assisted care centers and the like, what Elizabeth had in mind was the norm. My maternal great-grandfather lived with my grandparents for about fifteen years, until he was ninety, and they took care of him. That's how it was in a simpler time.

Today, with the cost of care rising higher, and as people live ever longer to face a wider array of illnesses and frailties, the old ways don't necessarily work. The children may have moved far away, busily balancing their careers and family lives. Logistically, they may be unavailable, and even if they were, would it be fair to saddle them with a responsibility that, more and more, requires clinical skills many simply don't possess? Caregiving can be onerous. It takes a toll physically, emotionally, and financially. Many people hesitate to burden their loved ones even when they would willingly help.

Clearly, a thorough retirement plan needs to weigh the potential that you will need long-term care, or custodial care, as I often call it to distinguish it from acute medical treatment. Everybody has a plan, even if it's "I'll just deal with it if it happens." Some people of sufficient wealth do intend to pay out-of-pocket, but most people need financial protection from this risk, which easily could wipe out their life savings.

Long-term care could cost hundreds of thousands of dollars. Why would you not do something to prepare for that possibility? You probably have homeowners insurance and auto insurance, even though you are not expecting your house to burn down and you probably won't total your car on the way to the supermarket. It only makes sense to protect against a financial risk that could be even more devastating.

My primary advice is this: Know your plan. Whether your plan is self-funding, traditional long-term care insurance, or an alternative approach, you should not be caught by surprise if you or your spouse faces this need. Like the other risks to your financial well-being, this one can be anticipated and effectively managed so that you need not worry about the unknown.

WHY NOT MEDICARE OR MEDICAID?

Some people fail to plan effectively because they think the government will take care of them if they should need custodial care. They believe that their life savings will be secure because the government has some big insurance policy that will cover them for a lifetime. They are wrong. In short, Medicare will cover next to nothing, and Medicaid won't kick in unless (or until) you're broke.

The Medicare system provides very little for extended care. It isn't designed for that purpose. Generally, it will pay only if you are transferred to an approved facility from the hospital for rehab care, and then only for about a hundred days, after which you will need to pay out-of-pocket or through whatever other insurance you have. By no means can you depend upon it to protect your retirement nest egg.

The state-based Medicaid system does pay for custodial care service, but you will be expected to use most of your own money first before the additional aid kicks in. Some people pursue a strategy in which they purposefully deplete their assets in advance so that they will be destitute on paper, thereby adding themselves to the rolls of an already overburdened system.

If you believe that's a good strategy, you must start such planning at least five years before you would expect to apply to enter a facility. The government will be watching. It will conduct a five-year "look back" to discover when assets were transferred to your family or others. If you give money away or try to put it in a trust within those five years, the government will presume you did so to qualify for coverage. You won't be deemed eligible until you contribute the amount of any such transfers toward your care.

Regulations vary by state, but generally you and your spouse will only be able to keep your house, car, personal belongings, and a small amount of other assets, with strict limits on permissible income. The assets within a qualified retirement plan might not exclude you from Medicaid coverage if you are already receiving your required minimum distribution; however, the distribution itself will be counted as income and may make you ineligible nonetheless.

Most people who have spent a lifetime saving for their future are not eager to spend down their assets just so they can qualify for a government program. They look to other strategies to protect themselves from this risk.

ASSET PROTECTION STRATEGIES

Even those who are affluent enough to pay out-of-pocket for custodial care must ask themselves why they would not take action to better protect their assets. Many people, whether of greater or lesser means, use insurance to leverage their money. In other words, why not spend $10,000 to avoid the prospect of spending $500,000? It can make sense to spend the former so that the latter goes to loved ones and not to a custodial care facility or nursing home. Think of it this way: If you could spend a dime instead of a dollar for the same thing, why would you willingly hand over the dollar? That is essentially what people who self-insure against custodial care costs are doing.

The negatives of traditional long-term care insurance are not hard to list. The premiums are not guaranteed and in many cases have increased significantly. Some policyholders have faced increases of 50 or 75 percent. A lot of insurance companies have gotten out of the business. When purchasing such a policy, you must be careful that you are working with a well-funded company that understands and manages the risk.

An often-voiced objection to traditional long-term care insurance is that you will never get those premiums back. You are spending money on something you may never need. The risk, however, is quite clear, as the statistics show. The National Association of Insurance Commissioners recently projected that about 35 percent of people who reach age sixty-five will enter a nursing home at some point and that 70 percent will need long-term care in some form. The average stay in a nursing home is a year. In the next forty years, the number of people age eighty-five and older will nearly triple—to more than 18 million—which is certain to mean more people will be needing long-term care.

If you object to paying premiums because that money will never come back to you, you could consider an alternative strategy that provides long-term care benefits, if needed, as part of a life insurance policy or annuity.

A life insurance policy, for example, might offer early distribution of the death benefit if the money is needed for long-term care. As an example, if you have a $1 million policy, the insurance company may allow you to withdraw $800,000 over five years (as long as you qualify). If you die without needing that care, then all the money goes to your heirs. Or you might get an annuity with an "income doubler;" if you qualify and need the money for long-term care, the insurance company will double your monthly cash payment on the annuity. As an example, an annuity may pay you $10,000 a year in lifetime income. If you qualify, the annuity company can double that amount to $20,000 a year (for a fixed period of time).

These types of insurance products help to take the sting out of paying those premiums. You get the custodial care coverage as an added benefit, but only if you need it; otherwise, your money is still working for you. That might seem generous of the insurance companies, but remember that nothing is free. All they are doing is accelerating what they probably would have had to pay you anyway. The death benefit is smaller than it would have been without the custodial care, but at least you won't feel as if you are shoveling dollars into a policy to no avail. It's a trade-off.

I expect that more and more options will become available. But if you aren't working with an advisor who provides comprehensive wealth management, you might not hear about them until it's too late.

HELP FOR VETERANS AND THEIR SPOUSES

If you are a veteran or a veteran's surviving spouse, and you need nursing home or in-home assistance, you may be eligible for the VA's Aid and Attendance benefit that covers certain unreimbursed and recurring medical expenses. The disabilities don't need to be service-related.

To qualify as a veteran, you must have served at least ninety days, with at least one of those days being during wartime. You or your surviving spouse must need help performing everyday activities such as eating, getting dressed, bathing, or using the bathroom. As of 2016, you cannot have more than $80,000 in assets other than your home and car.

The 2016 maximum benefit was $21,466 for an unmarried veteran, or $25,448 with one dependent. For an unmarried surviving spouse, the maximum was $13,794.[7]The size of your Aid and Attendance benefit will depend on your income (not including welfare benefits or Supplemental Security Income).

Here's an example of how it works: Let's say you're a single veteran getting $15,000 a year from Social Security and $10,000 from a pension, for a total income of $25,000. Your eligible unreimbursed medical expenses total $20,000 a year. When you subtract those expenses from your income, the result is $5,000. That's your countable income. Your maximum benefit as a single veteran is $21,466, but you would get $5,000 a year less than that, or $16,466.

AN ISSUE YOU MUST ADDRESS

However you choose to deal with it (if at all), you must recognize that the potential need for custodial care poses a significant threat to your life savings. The top fear in retirement is running out of money, and this cost is one of the main reasons that could happen. Our longer lives make these expenses increasingly likely.

Many people don't think about this concern, let alone talk about it. It's not easy to consider setting aside some of your hard-earned savings to pay for something that you hope and pray you will never

---

7 "Long-Term Care Benefits for Veterans and Surviving Spouses," Elder-
LawAnswers (January 11, 2017), http://www.elderlawanswers.com/
long-term-care-benefits-for-veterans-and-surviving-spouses-6158.

need. It's painful to imagine a time when you or your spouse will be growing frail and facing death, but you must not put off fully discussing these matters. In my visits to numerous nursing homes while helping veterans obtain their benefits, I observed firsthand why this aspect of planning is so critical.

I've found that if you have seen a parent or other loved one face this struggle, you're more likely to understand the urgency. If it didn't happen to your parents, you may think it won't happen to you. It very well could. A financial planner who cares about all aspects of your family's well-being will make sure you have dealt with this risk appropriately.

QUESTIONS TO CONSIDER

- What are the pros and cons of traditional long-term care insurance?
- Could it make sense to pay out-of-pocket if the need for custodial care arises?
- What part of these expenses will Medicare cover? What must you do if you want Medicaid to pay your way?
- How might you use life insurance or an annuity to protect against this risk?
- If you are a veteran, or if you married one, are you eligible for long-term care benefits?
- What is your plan for dealing with the high costs of medical and custodial care?

CREATING A LEGACY

Will your legacy be a burden or a blessing?

Estate planning is more than wills and trusts and tax strategies. Although those are highly important, this is about leveraging your dollars to leave a legacy for your loved ones and for the causes and institutions you care about. By enhancing your true wealth, you can have a bigger influence on the broader world.

As a schoolteacher for thirty-five years, Sam had done well, accumulating $1.5 million by age sixty-five. He was set to get a good pension and Social Security, on which he could easily live in comfort. It was a life savings he didn't really need, and so he resolved to leverage it to even greater heights for the next generation.

Specifically, Sam used a small part of his money to buy a life insurance policy inside of a properly structured trust. The payout upon his passing would be $5 million for his heirs, along with instructions on how it would be managed and spent. He could have just kept investing his money, at a return of perhaps 5 percent, but it's highly unlikely he ever could have parlayed it into $5 million. But that's what he was able to do through thoughtful planning that bridged generations. He saw the value in spending a relatively small amount of his money to create a legacy.

That's what is possible with careful estate planning. You can provide financial support for your children and grandchildren and for the causes and institutions that matter to you, and on top of that, you potentially can reduce your tax bill significantly all around.

When we talk about estate planning, we are talking about strategies for enhancing your true wealth. This is about more than money and investments. Wealthy people not only can take care of themselves but are able to affect the broader world. That could mean influencing family or helping the world through charitable contributions. A lot of people complain that the rich guys and the politicians call the shots, but even if you are of relatively modest means, you still can wield significant influence. If you plan properly, you can multiply the power of your money to create a lasting legacy. You can turn money into wealth.

So many people have squandered that opportunity. The singer Prince, who died recently from an accidental overdose of an opioid painkiller, left an estate estimated at about $300 million, not including the value of a vault of unpublished music. He died, however, without a will or a trust or any wealth transfer documents, so all his assets were scheduled for probate. Half of the estate value is expected to go to taxes.

This was a man intent on controlling his image and publicity and business affairs. The music vault had to be drilled open after Prince's death, because only he knew the lock combination. If properly planned for, it all would have passed smoothly to his chosen heirs without the costs, the delays, and the publicity of probate. He could have made sure those assets were managed as he desired. He did none of that. For lack of any meaningful planning, he ultimately lost all control over what would become of his treasures.

Prince is just one of the latest in a line of celebrities and notables whose estate messes have made the news, including Howard Hughes, James Brown, and Jimi Hendrix, to name a few from years past. The Michael Jackson estate became a billion-dollar tax battle. Many people—multimillionaires and regular folks alike—neglect estate planning, especially when they are in good health. There's always tomorrow, they figure, and along comes a tomorrow when it's too late.

And then there was the late Gene Wilder. He was a mainstay in our household since our daughter was five and fell in love with *Willy Wonka and the Chocolate Factory*. He married Saturday Night Live comedian Gilda Radner, who died of ovarian cancer. He then began to wind down his career and enjoyed a practical, planned retirement, actively promoting cancer awareness and treatment. I point to his example as a celebrity who recognized the meaning of wealth. He seemed to understand that we might not have tomorrow.

Before my mother died at seventy-two, she had seemed in good health, playing tennis daily. She had the basic estate documents, but we had not arranged to put her house in trust to reduce the taxes and charges that my sister and I would owe upon inheriting it as out-of-state residents. Our parents had bought the property in 1960 for $12,000. It had grown in value to $600,000. A family partnership or other measures could have saved tens of thousands of dollars. We were able to handle those estate expenses, but we could have managed it much better had we taken steps before her death.

It was a lesson that I took to heart and have passed on to the families I work with: Don't wait. Advance planning can save a fortune. Many families have been forced to sell businesses and properties when the tax bill comes due after the owner dies. If you explore all options, it need not be that way.

ESTATE PLANNING ESSENTIALS

The primary documents of estate planning include the following:

WILL

Your will is the basic document for passing assets to heirs. In it, you name an executor to pay final taxes and expenses and distribute your assets as you have specified. You also can name a guardian for minor children. Upon your death, the executor files your will in probate court, which oversees distribution and debt payments. The will does not take effect until death, however, so you need other estate tools to manage your assets if you become incapacitated.

REVOCABLE LIVING TRUST

A revocable trust provides for managing your financial affairs when you're alive, even if you're incapacitated, as well as upon death. The provisions can continue your influence for generations. The assets in your trust avoid the costs and publicity of probate. The terms provide for distribution of assets. While you are alive, you can change those provisions at any time, and if you act as your own trustee, you continue to manage your investments and financial affairs.

DURABLE POWER OF ATTORNEY

This document authorizes someone to act on your behalf if you are unable. You can limit the powers, but generally he or she can invest or spend your assets. It's a "durable" power because it continues if you're incapacitated, but not after your death.

HEALTH CARE POWER OF ATTORNEY

This separate document appoints someone to make medical decisions if you can't make them for yourself. When that's the case, conflict often divides families, and sometimes the courts must decide. By legally designating this trusted person in advance, you avoid such a rift.

ADVANCE MEDICAL DIRECTIVE

Often called a "living will," this document specifies whether doctors should take life-sustaining measures if you are permanently unconscious or terminally ill and can't speak for yourself. The directive does not necessarily give anyone else the right to speak for you, however; that's the function of the health care power of attorney.

THE CAPTAIN OF THE TEAM

Estate planning takes a team that includes your financial advisor, your accountant, and your estate attorney. Of those, your financial advisor likely will know you best. You probably see your accountant once a year, and your lawyer only when you need legal papers drawn up. They're good at what they do, but your financial advisor, if he or she is more than just an investment consultant, will know much more about what's important to you and the issues you face. Advisors know about your beneficiaries, whether you have a special-needs child, your goals and dreams, your family challenges, your health— not to mention the nature of your investments, which is of course an essential consideration in estate planning.

I recently was discussing estate matters with a woman with substantial assets and a generous heart who intended to leave it all to her sister or, if the sister wasn't alive, to her nieces and nephews. "Did you know, though," I asked her, "that in our state a niece or nephew is not considered a 'blood relative' and the taxes are considerably higher?" She was dumbfounded that her attorney hadn't told her that.

I wasn't surprised. Financial advisors learn a lot, because they do much of the advance and follow-up work. That's why it's critically important that your advisor knows not only how to invest your money but also will make sure it goes where you want it to go. Working with your other professionals, your advisor can serve as the captain of your team and ensure it all goes smoothly.

DIVVYING YOUR DOLLARS

Much is involved in deciding the best way to pass on your resources, whether to your spouse, to the next generation, or to charity. All dollars are not treated equally. If your heirs inherit a regular brokerage account, for example, they generally can figure taxes based on the value of the investments at the time of your death (rather than when originally purchased), resulting in a substantial savings for them on the capital gains. If you leave your children an IRA or 401(k)-type account, however, they don't get that "step-up" in the cost basis. They still owe those deferred taxes, and that inheritance will be added to their own income as either a lump sum or regular withdrawals, which likely will push them into the high tax brackets.

Another highly advantageous way to pass on your wealth is to leave what I call "leveraged dollars." Through life insurance, you may be able to leave several dollars to the next generation for every dollar you pay on the policy. And the money goes to your heirs "triple tax-free"—no capital gains tax, no income tax, and no estate tax. Folks often tell me, "I don't want to waste my money on life insurance." I explain that, to the contrary, they are magnifying their money.

I help them with those decisions and more. We work together to determine which accounts they should be using first as retirement income and which accounts make more sense to leave as a legacy, whether to family or charity. We make sure beneficiary designations are updated, because those take precedence over the wording of the will or trust. You don't want all your money to go to an ex-spouse simply because you neglected to review the papers. It happens.

Your goal in estate planning is to do the best you can for those who will follow you. Most people want control over those decisions rather than letting the government tax and spend as it sees fit. If you have tried to keep taxes down while you're alive, why wouldn't you want to keep them down after you die? Through diligent planning, it's within your power to divert more of your money to your loved ones and to the causes you find meaningful.

Creating a legacy is not just for the super-affluent. There are ways to turn even modest savings into true wealth. It's up to you. If you choose to let the government take half your money, then I say thanks for helping offset the national debt. Otherwise, you can do much to leave a personal legacy for your family and posterity. That's what most people choose to do—once they understand their options.

QUESTIONS TO CONSIDER

- What are the primary documents of estate planning?
- Do you have a complete set of estate documents prepared?
- Have you updated your estate documents in the last five years?
- Have you reviewed your beneficiary designations for your accounts in the last five years?
- Have you considered creating a legacy?

Chapter 10

ADVICE YOU CAN TRUST

Do you trust your advisor to manage your wealth?

Good guidance is critical in this new era of retirement planning. You need a specialist who knows how to make your money last, takes the time to get to know you and your situation, and acts only in your best interest. Beware of an advisor who has just one solution to all your complex needs. How is your advisor paid? Are there any conflicts of interest? In a fiduciary relationship, these must be fully disclosed. It's a matter of integrity.

J ohn and Theresa were a lovely couple, but the prospect of retiring had their nerves frazzled. Their anxiety was apparent as they sat down with me to review their finances. "Are we going to have enough? Is our money going to last? We just don't know."

I looked at their documents and asked a few questions. They had been living on a combined income of about $85,000 year, and it turned out that they had a $3.5 million portfolio. Earlier in his career, John had sold a business and set aside the proceeds in investments, never touching that money. He pursued a new career, and they were living off that income. Meanwhile, the investment account grew to a fortune.

"Let me suggest a possibility to you," I told the couple. "Let's say you were to invest your $3.5 million in high-quality municipal bonds, which could bring you a return of 4 percent. That would be a $140,000 tax-free income to you right there. On top of that, you would have your Social Security, and I see you have a bit of a pension coming your way." I did some calculations. "That totals $190,000 a year, much of it untaxed. Now, compare that with the $85,000 a year gross that you're bringing in today, before the taxes come out. Does that sound good to you? I'm not saying yet that's what we'll do, but it's a possibility. Do you like those figures?"

"Heavens, yes!" they said in unison, and the look on their faces showed me how deeply relieved they felt. "So we're going to be all right," Theresa added. "We did a great job!" I find it highly gratifying whenever I can help people see through the confusion and know that they will do well in retirement.

Let me point out that I make no money on the purchase of municipal bonds. I don't take a commission or a spread. Had I been working in my own interest instead of theirs, I instead could have tried to earn a hefty commission. I don't operate that way. I'm not driven to offer advice based on whether I can profit from a product. I offer advice based on what makes sense and is in your best interest.

A SKILLED OARSMAN

After reading this book, you probably realize that we are in a new age of retirement planning. Therefore, it only makes sense that anyone who has money should seek professional guidance—and the right kind of guidance. It is much easier to accumulate and grow money than it is to wisely preserve and distribute it during retirement. It is easier to build a portfolio than it is to make it last. You need to work with someone who has expertise in the latter. Choosing that person is perhaps your most important decision in ensuring a successful retirement.

Imagine you are going white-water rafting. It's a tranquil day, and you step into the raft on the sandy shore and drift out into the current. You and your boat mates proceed slowly and smoothly at first, but then the boat picks up speed as you approach the rapids. Soon you are holding on for dear life, rushing downriver amid the rocks. At that moment, who's the most important person in the boat? You'd probably agree it's whoever is steering. That's who will get you through this. Your oarsman is the one who understands the river and its ways.

When you choose your guide, you will want somebody who understands your river—who knows how to get around the rocks on the stretch you're preparing to travel. You don't want a rookie. You want an experienced navigator who has skillfully dealt with these challenges before, with many people just like you. This is a river unlike the others you have known, with different obstacles and opportunities up ahead. The ride should feel thrilling, not threatening.

Unless you have someone steering whom you can trust, you will be alone at the oars. Unless you engage someone with expertise in managing money for retirement, it will all be up to you. Many people do feel up to the task of managing their money, choosing funds and anticipating where the market is heading. Some actually stay afloat.

IN YOUR BEST INTEREST

As a registered investment advisor, I have a fiduciary duty to do what is best for my clients and to always put their interests before my own. I am required by law—and by integrity—to operate by that standard and to disclose any conflict of interest. My allegiance is to the family that I represent. That is the type of relationship that you should expect from your financial advisor.

Investments are not simply good or bad; rather, they are appropriate or inappropriate, depending upon the situation. Let's look at a fact of investment life: Advisor A warns people to put all their money in annuities so as not to lose any of it, while Advisor B warns people to put all their money in the market and not waste it on annuities. Consider how they make their money. The annuity salesperson makes money when you buy annuities. The market advocate wants to get more of your money into the market so he or she can make more on it.

But how could either of those advisors really have your best interest in mind when they are taking an entire class of investments off the table before they even get to know you? Once a qualified advisor gets to know you and your personal situation, the investment approach should become obvious. The appropriate choice should be clear. Every investment is designed for a purpose. It serves a specific function in a comprehensive plan that is customized to the individual family. Trust your gut: If you don't understand the investment, maybe it's not right for you.

WHO HAS YOUR BACK?

I have learned through the years that many people—who are otherwise highly sophisticated, with abundant expertise in their fields—don't recognize the difference between a Wall Street broker, insurance salesperson, and an advisor who truly will protect their interests.

In fact, financial literacy in general is often lacking, even among those who have attained success in life. We have no formal financial education in this country. What is taught in the colleges is all theoretical. The professionals learn to invest by doing it. The financial services industry is based on apprenticeship. If you want to be a good investment advisor, you work for an investment advisor. There is no substitute for experience. The market crashes of 2001 and 2008, for example, demolished portfolios but greatly expanded awareness.

And there is much to learn. Some people feel intimidated and vulnerable, the way they might feel when buying a car from a polished salesperson who moves twenty cars a month and knows much more about how the game is played. Nonetheless, professional guidance is crucial for those who aspire to financial success in retirement.

There are some things you can't effectively do yourself. They require a breadth of knowledge and experience. Most people, for example, understand the folly of trying to diagnose their own physical ailments. They don't try to pull their own teeth, and they hire a lawyer if they are going to court for anything other than a traffic ticket. And yet they hesitate to seek a financial diagnosis. Often it's because they fear they will appear foolish about money, and so they don't ask for help even as their situation worsens.

They may feel suspicious about the entire industry. It's true that there have been many people in the financial world operating like car salesmen. But others don't. How, then, can you tell the difference? How do you know whether your advisor truly has your back?

I believe it's a matter of what the advisor is doing behind the scenes. Advice doesn't come free, of course, and your advisor certainly will want to be compensated. The question is where that money comes from. Are the fees fully disclosed and transparent? If commissions are being paid, are you aware of them? Some advisors have long worn two hats: one moment the fiduciary hat, the next the sales hat.

Many people in the financial industry get their money through such methods as revenue sharing and soft dollar arrangements. In essence, a mutual fund company or insurance company is paying the broker or advisor to use their investments over other, potentially better options. These are not illegal arrangements, but they are not necessarily in your best interest. When recommending an investment strategy, a fiduciary advisor must disclose all the good and the bad and what he or she is earning on the transactions. You should get a clear explanation as to what is happening with your money.

Beware of anyone who seems to have only one solution to any problem. It is as if a doctor hands you a vial and says, "Just drink this, it will take care of anything that ails you." They may be bright, helpful, and remarkably friendly, but they have only one solution for you because that is how they make their money. They don't want anything or anyone else to lure you away.

You should always be wary of anything that sounds too good to be true. How, for example, could anyone guarantee you a return of 7 percent when Treasury bonds are only paying 2 percent? A couple recently came in for a visit and announced that their neighbors had told them about some amazing investment that would yield 14 percent in the first year, followed by a guaranteed 5 percent for the next decade. It doesn't require much financial sophistication to realize that in today's interest rate environment, something is a little fishy there.

If advisors who claim to be making a living in the financial industry are telling you that you are getting a remarkable deal at no cost to you, then how do they keep the lights on in their house? How can they afford to drive that nice car? How can financial professionals offer you something for free when they need your money to make money? Somehow, they are getting paid, and that's all right—as long as they explain what they are doing and as long as you're comfortable with it. You want to be working with someone who is knowledgeable, who creates a plan that meets your needs, and who is upfront about how he or she gets paid. You need to be clear about whose interests the advisor will be serving.

IN SEARCH OF SOUND ADVICE

For years, I have heard the tales at cocktail parties about someone's phenomenal success at choosing some stock or another that skyrocketed into a fortune. Never, however, have I ever been approached by anyone eager to tell me about a big loser. You would think that the world abounds with Wall Street wizards. If they were that good, wouldn't they be summering in Monaco?

My point is that you need to be careful about accepting advice from neighbors, friends, coworkers, long-winded uncles, or anyone with a glowing face who seems to possess the key to your dreams. Aside from the likelihood that those folks might very well be full of baloney, they probably don't know all that much about your personal situation. And frankly, they are not you. Most will be in a different stage of life, such as their early accumulation years, when they might be able to endure more of a high-rolling risk to the portfolio. If you are sixty-five years old, why would you feel that the glib twenty-six-year-old at the water cooler has any answers that in any way apply to what would be best for you? You are heading for retirement after work. That kid is probably heading for the bar after work to find someone else to tell tall tales.

There's no shortage of sources for bad financial advice, and many people seem very willing to accept it. My guess is they wouldn't accept medical advice from their plumber, but they're doing something similar when they go to the wrong kind of professional for counsel.

My cousin is a dermatologist. Knowing he's a doctor, people often approach him to ask about a spot on their hand or a persistent itch in the armpit. "So what do you think, doc?" they ask him. And he is consistent in telling them that he doesn't know. They would have to come in for a close examination and a full analysis of their health. He needs a medical history. Any other response would be highly unprofessional. An on-the-spot diagnosis would be unconscionable. He's not going to say, "Gosh, looks like cancer!"

I sometimes tell folks that story if they come through my door and, within minutes, are fishing for some hot stock tip that will make them rich. Before they choose anything, I tell them they need a full analysis of their personal and financial situation, because any other response would be highly unprofessional. Sometimes they ask, right at the gate, whether they should buy an annuity, and like my dermatologist cousin, I tell them that I would need to know more. It might be appropriate for some people in some measure, but it would be a terrible choice for others. So much depends upon age and expectations, and I would not presume to weigh in on the matter without a full financial workup. I need to do that exam. I need a history, so I'll be asking questions. You can tell whether an advisor is right for you by the kind of questions he or she asks .

Most financial vehicles can be put to good use to solve the right problem for the right person. Used unwisely, they backfire. I don't like mutual funds, for example, and might feel that you can do better with other types of investments, but I wouldn't say they're bad for everybody. Instead, I'll point out the good points and the bad, and together we'll determine which outweighs the other. Beware of comments such as "all annuities are bad" or "stay away from the stock market" or "Bank CDs are horrible." Sometimes they are, and sometimes they're not. Blanket condemnations or endorsements of an investment class are far from helpful.

What you will hear from the media is not particularly helpful, either. Just like the coworkers at the water cooler, those columnists and commentators know nothing about you. They are producing information for consumption by the masses, and what they have to say may be skewed by commercial interests. The advice you read in a magazine or hear from a talking head on the television may very well include a dose of financial wisdom, but what you truly need goes far beyond investments. You need a Wealth Strategy that will specifically serve your family for years to come, in any kind of market or economic climate, with your personal goals always top of mind.

Though you may feel tempted to rely upon online resources, be aware of how search engines can be manipulated and information can be skewed. Marketers can target you so that you receive certain pitches that lead you toward their wares. Many people do not bring a great deal of discernment to those search results, and the sheer volume is daunting. How can you be expected to sift through it all to find the nuggets? There certainly is no personal touch in those search results. They are not designed to meet your individual situation, and without that, any "advice" is of questionable value.

TRUST AND COMPATIBILITY

Every financial professional should be able to clearly express and explain a worldview that you can compare with your own. That's how you will determine whether you're a good fit for a relationship that could continue for decades. Such a relationship requires the development of a rapport and the building of trust, or you won't be able to accomplish much together.

Your financial advisor should be much more than someone who buys and sells for you. You need someone who is compatible with you. If you tend to be an aggressive investor who is willing to take risks, then you will be looking for the type of advisor who manages that way—within reason. As for me, I emphasize the preservation of your money so that it can generate income while growing at a conservative pace. That is my view, and those who choose to work with me have a similar outlook. If you clearly aren't cut from that cloth, I will tell you up front that someone else might be better suited for the job.

Those who do choose to work with me can be confident that they are fully in control. They have not lost authority over their financial life. Rather, they have gained a level of expertise. It is ironic that those who feel concerned about losing their authority have no problem putting their money into a mutual fund, where they really do lose control. By contrast, investments in a separately managed account are far more transparent.

Whenever you are going into unfamiliar territory, the smart thing to do is to hire a guide who knows the lay of the land, the best trails, and the dangers lurking in the underbrush. I am such a guide. I can cut a good path through the jungle. I can maneuver that raft around the rocks when the waters get wild.

Speaking of waters, I like to tell the tale of the day my BMW stalled out on a flooded roadway during a storm in Pennsauken, New

Jersey. Other cars were getting through, so I tried, too—and I learned a few things that day. For one, nobody with low-profile tires should try to drive through even an inch of water. And, as the water rose, I also learned this: BMWs float. So I learned the hard way that day. The car was totaled, and I had owned it only a month. If someone with any experience in driving BMWs had been sitting beside me, I could have steered clear. It was a day that I truly could have used a good guide myself.

Investors, too, need a good guide. They need someone to help steer them clear of their own emotions, for one thing. The same thing happens to them that happens so often on sports teams: An up-and-coming young player gets a big contract, and the team holds on to him not only as he reaches his peak but also as he begins his inevitable decline. The team would do far better to trade that player when he is at his best, so as not to get stuck with him. Instead, the team keeps him through hell or high water, reluctant to part with the one-time star.

Investors often behave that way, too. They need an advisor who can help them make rational and unbiased decisions about their money. Frankly, they need an advisor who is willing to help save them from themselves—who can see what they cannot see, because they are too emotionally invested in the investments.

Everyone has an advisor. If you are not working with a financial professional, your advisor is the person staring back at you when you look into the mirror. Perhaps you are qualified to do all of it yourself. Just ask yourself this: Would you hire that person in the mirror to handle the full range of your financial affairs? Your ego might say "yes." Common sense likely will tell you that you should delegate to someone with the experience and expertise to lead you in the right directions.

MY TWO PROMISES

Let me share with you my approach so that you might compare it with that of other advisors. Whenever people come to my office for a consultation, I can make them two promises. One is that by the time they leave, they will know more about their financial situation than they did before they came to me. They will be better equipped to make the key decisions that will determine the course of their retirement. I can help them to gain the perspective they need to plan productively. They will have a better idea about where they stand.

I don't pressure anyone to become a client, and that is a decision they will make at the end of the first meeting. We need to get to know each other to make sure we're a good fit. Both of us need that assurance, and that can only come about through open and forthright discussion. I tell you exactly what I believe, based upon what I see at that point and how I assess your situation. Though a lot of work remains to be done, it must all be built on a foundation of utter honesty. And that is my second promise to all who enter my doors: I will be straight with them.

That's my personal formula for business success. I know that by keeping those promises, my financial practice will thrive. My goal is to educate people—to be their guide through this new territory, to be the financial coach who brings out their best. My purpose is to equip people with the tools to build a financial house that will keep them secure for a lifetime. I know that if I do that consistently, I will have plenty of business.

QUESTIONS TO CONSIDER

- ♀ How does your advisor earn his or her compensation?

- ♀ Does your advisor serve any interests other than what is best for you?

- ♀ How much does your advisor understand about your situation and aspirations?

- ♀ Does your advisor have extensive experience in working with people transitioning into retirement?

- ♀ Do your advisor's views feel compatible with your own?

- ♀ Is your advisor forthright in telling you both the good and the bad of your financial prospects?

- ♀ Is your advisor a fiduciary who is required by law to put your interests first?

Conclusion

INTO A PROSPEROUS RETIREMENT

I f you ever have gone on a road trip with children, I'm sure you have heard the incessant chorus of "are we there yet?" from the back seat. They know they're going somewhere exciting, but they don't quite know how to measure their progress in getting there.

"We'll be there in seventy-five miles," you might tell them, just to hear the same question a few minutes later. A better answer would be, "You'll know when you see the ocean," or, "Just look for Mickey's ears!" That way they can picture the destination. They have a vision, not just a number.

If you can't imagine where you're going in retirement, you are like the kids in the car. How do you know when you're "there?" What does it look like? When I ask folks that, I usually get a financial answer. They respond in terms of how much money they will need so they can retire. It's a numbers answer, not a destination answer.

If you don't know where you're going, you certainly won't get there. And if you do have a destination, you must figure out where you are now, so you can map your course. You need a good guide. There will be many forks in the road, so you should travel with someone who has seen where every path leads.

You deserve more than the numbers game. Your life should have texture and color and context as you pursue what matters most to you. Your goal, above all, should be a happy and successful retirement. Money matters, but it's a means to the end. It's not the end.

In every chapter of this book, I hope you have heard this message: You need a Wealth Strategy, not just an investment strategy. As we live ever longer, retirement money must last for decades and outpace inflation. Taxes have become a huge issue for everyone in this post-pension era of 401(k) plans. Our longer lives also dramatically increase health care costs and the potential need for long-term care. Wealth advisors, who will help you work through all those concerns and more, make up only a few percent of the ranks of financial professionals. I'm proud to be in that number.

Despite the challenges, many families have done a great job accumulating wealth. It's often said that you can't take it with you, but you can leave plenty behind to ensure generations of financial security in these uncertain times. That's the mark of true wealth.

It's what you don't know that will hurt you. Much of the investment business is built around the promotion of ignorance, and my goal is to teach people about all the aspects of their financial lives that, together, make up a comprehensive Wealth Strategy. Knowledge will protect you and take you to greater heights. That is what I have shared with you in these pages. It's what you need to know for real success and a prosperous retirement. You won't have to wonder whether you're there yet. You'll have arrived.

Your Wealth Strategy Checklist

TO BE SUCCESSFUL IN RETIREMENT
YOU MUST HAVE A STRATEGY!

1. Create vision for your retirement.

2. Plan for a long life.

3. Determine what type of financial advice you want and need.

4. Determine the type of advisor you want to work with.

5. Create a budget for essential and nonessential spending.

6. Document guaranteed income for retirement, such as Social Security.

7. Create a personal balance sheet that includes all assets and liabilities.

8. Identify which liabilities will be paid off before retirement.

9. Using items 3, 4, 5, and 6, determine your income deficit.

10. Using your current assets and income deficit, determine your minimum rate of return.

11. Evaluate your personal risk profile.

   ♥ Capacity

   ♥ Attitude

   ♥ Need

12. Evaluate your current investments.

   ♥ What is your current level of risk?

   ♥ What is your current level of volatility?

   ♥ What would happen to your plan if the worst happens in one year?

13. Evaluate your tax risk.

   ♥ Divide your assets into tax buckets.

   ♥ Determine your potential tax costs for your tax-deferred accounts.

14. Establish a baseline for inflation.

15. Using all that you have learned, create an income plan.

16. Using all that you have learned, develop an investment strategy to match your needs.

17. Evaluate your healthcare costs and long-term care needs.

18. Create or update your estate plan.

Get started today. Manage, monitor, and adjust on a regular basis. Enjoy a long and successful retirement!

TFG Wealth Management LLC

O ur mission is to help you make the vision of your future a reality through comprehensive wealth management and advice.

Our firm works with business owners, families, and individuals who need help managing their wealth or are preparing for retirement. Using our proprietary wealth strategy approach we will help you to and through retirement.

We strongly recommend that you start with our complimentary second opinion services. Our team will work with you to develop your vision for the future, analyze your current financial situation, determine if you are on the right path, explain your investments (what they are, how they work, what your fees are), and discuss options to improve your financial plan.

Our review includes:

- an income analysis where we look at longevity, inflation, Social Security optimization, and cash-flow requirements

- ♥ a tax review where we look at the potential impact of your required minimum distributions

- ♥ an investment risk review where we analyze the risk you are currently taking and measure it against what you expect

- ♥ an investment stress test where we use twenty-first-century technology to project potential outcomes for your investments based on different financial and economic scenarios

- ♥ a custodial care review where we look at the impact of assisted living and nursing home costs on your financial plan

- ♥ an estate and legacy review where we explore options that you may not have thought of for transferring your wealth from one generation to another

Depending on your circumstances, some or all of these issues will be addressed by a team member during your complimentary consultation.

Call 215-999-1919 or email us at info@tfgwealth.com.